Reach Out

Building Relationships That Actually Matter

Marc Zawrotny

Copyright © 2025 Marc A. Zawrotny

All rights reserved.

No part of this book may be reproduced, distributed, or transmitted in any form or by any means, including photocopying, recording, or other electronic or mechanical methods, without the prior written permission of the publisher, except in the case of brief quotations used in reviews, articles, or other noncommercial uses permitted by copyright law.

For information, visit: **www.marczawrotny.com**

ISBN 979-8-9936935-0-7 (paperback)

First Edition

Cover illustration © Madison Zawrotny

Published by *Paranomus Press*

Printed in the United States of America

This is a work of nonfiction. Names and identifying details have been changed in some cases to protect the privacy of individuals.

Cover Art

Illustration by Madison Zawrotny

Madison Zawrotny is a freelance illustrator and designer who graduated from Ringling College of Art and Design. Her work blends expressive color, character-driven storytelling, and imaginative worldbuilding — often exploring emotion and human connection through vibrant, stylized imagery.

Her portfolio and artwork can be found under **@recklesssketches** on Instagram and through **redbubble.com/people/recklesssketches.**

*To my wife and soulmate Melissa—
without whom I would not have grown
into the person I am today.*

Acknowledgements

I have a lot of people to thank—those who have been part of this book, supported my work, and are simply awesome in general.

Family

Starting at the top: the best person in the world I could possibly have had the fortune to marry, my wife, **Melissa**. My most important connection… bar none.

To my wonderful mom, **Barbara**, who has always believed in me and continues to be such a big part of my life.

To my kids, **Nicolas** and **Shannon**, through whom I've learned how connection evolves across generations.

And not to be ignored, my extremely talented niece, **Madison Zawrotny**, who created this book's cover art!

Friends and Colleagues

Thank you to:

Jacob Welp, CEO of Rapport (https://rapport.tax/) and good friend, without whom I wouldn't have survived being laid off. I've learned so much from you. I'm blessed to have you in my life.

John Orsanic, mentor and friend, who has the best laugh in the business.

Simon Zatyrka, chef, podcaster, and mentor, who told me exactly what I needed, exactly when I needed it.

To the colleagues and mentors who shared lessons that stayed with me for years—your impact is reflected throughout these pages, even if the stories have been adjusted to protect privacy. You all mean so much to me.

For everyone else I haven't mentioned, please know that your support has been amazing and not forgotten. It would take another whole book to thank you all.

And I'm especially grateful to those joining me as early readers. Your feedback helps shape not just this book, but how I share these ideas with the world.

Table of Contents

Introduction i

Section I: Understanding Connection 1

Chapter 1: Why Connection Matters 2

Chapter 2: The Curse of Digital Depersonalization 6

Chapter 3: Your Words vs. Their Feelings: Intent and Interpretation 11

Chapter 4: Emotional Intelligence and Connection 14

Chapter 5: Connection in Times of Change 21

Section II: Building the Habit 26

Chapter 6: Building Habits Around Staying in Touch 27

Chapter 7: Tools of the Trade – Phones, Calendars, & Contact Lists 34

Chapter 8: Consistency Is King (or Queen) 44

Chapter 9: Don't Waste the Wait 49

Chapter 10: Managing Your Energy and Expectations 58

Chapter 11: When Connection Is One-Sided 63

Chapter 12: Follow Up or Fade Away 68

Chapter 13: Why Responding Still Matters 73

Chapter 14: The Power of Small Gestures 76

Chapter 15: Storytelling as a Connector's Secret Weapon 83

Chapter 16: Connecting Through Humor and Vulnerability .. 90

Section III: Connection at Work 95

Chapter 17: Connection in the Workplace – Why It's More Than Just a Job..96

Chapter 18: Connecting with Your Boss and Executives.......105

Chapter 19: Top Down - Leading with Connection................126

Chapter 20: Inside-Out: Becoming Comfortable in Your Own Skin..139

Chapter 21: Working Across Departments and Functions...143

Chapter 22: The Power of Curiosity and Good Questions...152

Section IV: Leaving a Legacy....................... 159

Chapter 23: Connection as a Form of Legacy.........................160

Chapter 24: Mentorship and Long-Term Relationship Building 166

Chapter 25: The Future Needs You: Connection in an AI World 175

The Connector's Field Guide....................... 184

Introduction

Why I Wrote This Book

I have to credit someone I met only in the last couple of years with giving me the push that led to what you're about to read. We were on a video call, and I was rambling about what I wanted to do with my life versus what I'd done as a career. My friend stopped me and cut through all the cobwebs life throws in to make things hard to see.

He said, "Marc, if you had your druthers, forgetting all considerations of money, etc.—what would you do? I don't care if you say you'd want to sell carved wooden ducks on the internet, what would you want to do most?"

Yes, he really used the word "druthers." If that's not in your vocabulary (or if you haven't been reading Charles Dickens lately), it just means "if you had your choice."

I didn't even hesitate: "Speak in public."

He leaned back in his chair and said, "Well, there you go."

I left that call with a new clarity… for about a minute.

Great, I thought. *I want to speak to people.*

That led me to thinking—maybe I should figure out what I'd actually speak about. I'd been told many times that my ability to connect with people is my superpower, and I knew how much I enjoyed working with people.

So I decided to write about it and eventually, that writing became the basis of this book.

My purpose in writing isn't to turn people into me. Ask my wife—one of me is more than enough.

I wrote this for anyone who wants to get just a little better at keeping in touch. That might mean deepening relationships you already have, or reaching out to people you'd like to know. Work, in particular, can be tough to navigate, so my goal was to give you some structure, tools, and ideas you can use—if they fit you.

There's truth in the old saying, "It's not what you know, it's who you know." My hope is that this book helps you build stronger relationships, optimize how you connect at work, and create that all-important network.

But I'd also add this: "who you know" only works if they know you. Collecting Facebook friends or LinkedIn contacts isn't enough. It's about having genuine connections with people you can talk to, vent with, ask advice from, and gain the benefit of their wisdom and experience — as you, in turn, share yours with others.

Connection is all about quality over quantity.

And I can tell you from experience: I've received so much joy and energy from staying in touch with people over the years. If that's something you want, too, then I hope these pages give you a few useful steps along the way.

Who This Book Is For

This book is for anyone who has ever said, *"I wish I could be better at keeping in touch."* It's for people who want to feel more comfortable and social in public, who want to find more joy in their work relationships, and who are looking for paths forward in building lasting connections.

And that's why I felt it was important to write about connection itself—because it touches every part of our lives.

How to Use This Book

You don't need to read straight through, though I set it up to flow that way if you want. Start wherever you need the most help—whether that's getting started, keeping consistency, making the most of workplace connections, or thinking about the legacy you leave behind.

At the end, you'll find *The Connector's Field Guide,* which pulls together all the tools in one place for easy reference. Use what works for you. Leave the rest. This is your journey.

Why Write About Connection

Our society has become much more insular than it used to be. Where making friends came easily as a kid, it's much harder as an adult. Granted, there are more demands on our time, responsibilities increase, and so on.

But think on this: would you rather watch a game on TV at home alone, or at a restaurant or bar surrounded by fellow fans? The experience changes, doesn't it?

The shared experiences we have in life are the ones we remember most. They become part of us and turn into favorite stories. Shared activities become deeper memories and cherished experiences. Connection makes everything better.

And truthfully, there are very few things in life that anyone can accomplish alone. Whether it's a work team, an executive sponsor, or a caring parent or grandparent, we do and become our best when we're supported by the company of positive connections.

Why Now

I believe this book could not have been written by me at any time before now. When I was younger, I didn't have the experience or wisdom. Later in life I was caught up in the corporate world, married, and raising two young children.

It wasn't until I was laid off that I finally had the space to stop and reflect. To write this, I needed the 30+ years of work and life — the stories (good and bad), the observations, and the nuggets of wisdom imparted by wiser folks along the way.

I also believe this book is timely. With social media, entertainment at our fingertips, and the emerging technology of AI, it is more important than ever to be seen as a real person rather than just a digital footprint.

Now that it's written, know this: it is truly a labor of love. I had so much fun working on it, and I hope that joy comes through as you read.

What's Ahead

This book is not a textbook. Far from it. It looks at connection through a lens of observations, solid advice, and personal experience over 30+ years. It's filled with stories, examples, tools, and practical ways to build and strengthen relationships.

If you're looking for more joy, energy, and opportunity from the people in your life and around you every day, then I believe you'll enjoy this read. Connection doesn't have to be complicated. It just has to be real.

Thanks, and Be Well!

Marc Zawrotny

Section I: Understanding Connection

I've found that you only really stick with things that mean something to you. For connection to become something important, then it should be evaluated to see where it fits in for your life. We'll look at examining why it matters in general, what it means to you, and even some ideas on how you can get started on identifying it so that you're clear on it for yourself. Then, you'll be ready to put connection into action.

Chapter 1: Why Connection Matters

When was the last time someone texted you out of the blue just to check in?
No pressing need or agenda. Nothing to ask of you. Simply, "Hey, I was thinking about you."

In a world of constant texts, notifications, messaging apps, and work demands, that kind of message can feel like a breath of fresh air. It isn't about action, it's about feeling. It says someone cares enough to pause and reach out.

The funny (or sad) thing is, most people don't send messages like that. I think they mean to. But those good intentions get buried under the noise. They get distracted. They assume the other person is probably busy, or worse, just wouldn't care.

That's the gap this book is here to close.

I wrote this because I kept hearing the same thing over and over: "I'm so bad at keeping in touch."
Usually said right after I'd reached out and they replied, "You're so good at this."

Here's the good news: it's not a personality flaw. It's a skill. A set of habits. And like any habit, connection is something you can build, even if you're not naturally extroverted or "a people person."

To be clear, this isn't just about being social. Connection shapes our friendships, our careers, our mental health, and even our sense of purpose. When we feel connected, we show up differently. We lead better. We listen better. We laugh more.

That's why this chapter…and this book…start here.

So, let's talk about connection, shall we?

Being able to relate and connect with other fellow human beings touches into all aspects of life.

It's how we make friends.
It's how we build relationships.
It's how we find love — and how we grow in our work..

Connecting seems easier when we're younger and harder as we get older. Seems is the operative word here. Truth is, connecting can be difficult at all ages.

Sometimes a great way to understand how important something is… is to imagine what life is like without it.

The pandemic gave us a stark reality check to how that could be. People sequestered and cut off from their friends and families into separate and very closed off spaces. A lot of people struggled…mentally, emotionally and physically.

That's an extreme case, sure. But I think it reminded us what we've been taking for granted most of our lives:

People matter.

We're wired for connection.

We NEED each other.

Only recently, after hearing, 'You're so much better at this, thanks for reaching out,' about a hundred times, I started to wonder…

Now, I know I genuinely enjoy connecting with people. I've always (if you don't count the first 16 years) been one of those people who gains energy from being around others. But I also know that's not true for everyone.

So, I started wondering, what if I could help? What could I share that people could use to be better at connecting... if they wanted to?

(That last part is the key.)

Not by changing who people are, but by sharing a few habits and mindsets that have worked for me.

This book is for anyone who wants to be a little better at staying in touch. Whether it's reconnecting with a friend, deepening relationships at work, or just feeling a little less isolated in your everyday life, my goal is to give you ideas and encouragement that help you feel more connected to your community, your world... and probably most importantly...yourself.

Connection doesn't have to be grand, or complicated, or saved for "important" people or moments.
It lives in how we show up, in the little things we do, say, and notice.

Throughout this book, we'll look at some of those aspects and places to connect. I'll cover ideas, habits, and even give you a toolkit to help you keep the momentum going.

For instance:

- What it means to have presence and awareness
- Workplace connection: How to build bridges at work
- Creating habits that build trust
- The emotional complexity of connection – what do you do when connection feels one-sided?

So, if connection is all around us, and it's not that complicated...

Why does it still feel so hard?

One big reason is what I call digital depersonalization.

Let's dive into what that means…and why it's quietly happening all around us.

Chapter 2: The Curse of Digital Depersonalization

What is digital depersonalization?

It's a term I coined, and honestly, I'm kind of proud of it.

It describes the shift we've made from human-centered direct communication to interface-centered communication through a medium.

We text more than we talk. We might instant message more than we text. Calling someone? That's practically a social faux pas. Talking face-to-face? Only if we have to.

Our devices have become the middlemen. And the people on the other end? They're often reduced to avatars, notification bubbles, or profile pictures they haven't changed since 2012.

We're more "connected" than ever... but also more disassociated from each other at the same time.

When every interaction is filtered through a screen, it's easy to forget there's a real person on the other end.

And once we forget that, things start to slip.

We assume, we judge, we forget to follow up.
Or worse... we just stop caring at all.

Have you ever gotten a text or email, maybe from a coworker, where the tone just rubbed you the wrong way?

And suddenly... you didn't like the person who sent it?

I'd bet yes.

Why does that happen?

Because of something I've learned the hard way over years of digital communication:

The written word is interpreted by the emotions of the reader—not the intention of the writer.

Let that sink in.

You might have meant something one way, but if the person reading it is tired, stressed, annoyed, or just had a bad morning... it lands differently. The message you thought you sent isn't the one they received.

Let me give you a simple example:

Me: Hey honey, how are you doing today?
Wife: Fine.

Now... does "fine" mean things are actually fine?
(Every married person reading this just tensed up a little.)
Or is "fine" code for "you should probably figure out what you did wrong"?

In this case, I pressed for more details. Turned out, she really was fine. We laughed about it later on a phone call—especially since in our house, now if my wife says she's "peachy," then I know there's trouble.

Every couple or family has their own version of this, but the takeaway is universal:

How you interpret a message depends on how well you know the person.

If you don't know them well? You fill in the blanks with assumptions.

And that's how it starts.

You read someone's short reply and assume they're annoyed.
You don't clarify. You don't ask.
You just… respond. Usually with your own energy—your own defensiveness, your own judgment.

And in that moment, they stop being a person. They become just "what they wrote."

That's digital depersonalization.

So where do we see this ALL THE TIME? The job market.

Think about it: a résumé is a flat summary of your experience. Sure, it lists what you've done, but does it tell someone how you work? Whether you're collaborative? How you lead under pressure? How you treat others?

Nope. It's just a highlight reel.

And now, with automated systems scanning those résumés before a human even sees them, it's not just depersonalized, it's practically dehumanized.

You become a keyword match, a file to be filtered, not a person to be understood.

That's serious digital depersonalization.

So how do you combat such an insidious foe?

The more connected you are with someone, the more likely they are to read your message as you intended, not as they're feeling. If you've experienced this, then it seems like you can actually hear them talking in your head, vs it being just plain text. Fact is, when you can hear the written communication as a person, then you know you're doing alright.

Here's a story of when this concept really hit hard for me:

The Person Behind the Email

I had this situation once with a colleague at a corporate office. They'd send these emails that always felt a little condescending. Demanding. Like they were barking orders from a keyboard.

I decided. I didn't like this person, and I'd never even spoken to them.

As a result, I'd drag my feet on fulfilling their requests. I was demotivated, and I'm sure they were frustrated.
Nobody won.

Then one day, already in a mood, another email came in, and I decided I was done. I picked up the phone, fully ready to give them a piece of my mind.

They answered on the first ring.

And instead of the power-trip tone I expected, I heard, "I'm so glad you called! I've been meaning to reach out to you."

I was floored.

We talked. He apologized for how his emails might have sounded and explained the urgency behind them. I finally understood where he was coming from. I hung up that call realizing... he wasn't a jerk at all. He was just trying to get something done. Quickly. But through email, it had all felt cold, abrasive, and one-sided.

That phone call changed everything.

Because after that time, when I got an email from him, I didn't just see the words, I heard him. I knew the voice behind the message. I knew his intent. He was no longer a signature block in my inbox. He was a person.

When we lose the person behind the message, everything gets harder, collaboration, empathy, and especially trust.
But the moment we reconnect on a human level, the whole dynamic can shift.

That's why we have to fight digital depersonalization.
And that's exactly what this book is here to help you do.

Chapter 3: Your Words vs. Their Feelings: Intent and Interpretation

As a child of the 80s, I've seen incredible advances in communication technology. Yes, I'm one of those people who can say, "I remember before the internet" (that's the 21st century equivalent of the walking to school in the snow uphill both ways but from the generation before), back when you had to find a payphone instead of pulling one from your pocket.

That said, I'm not someone who wishes for a return to the "good old days." Life changes. Technology changes. And I've watched it shift firsthand… as a parent of two adult children, I've seen how phones and social media have reshaped how people connect.

What I've noticed is this: the social needs we had growing up: belonging, popularity, friendship. They're all still the same today.

But everything moves faster.

Feedback is instant.
Conflict is quicker.
Misunderstandings travel at the speed of Wi-Fi (provided you have over three bars).

When I was younger, if someone upset you, you had to go talk to them face-to-face. Or at the very least, call them. That meant you saw their body language, heard their tone, felt their presence. The phone removed visuals, but still preserved emotion.

How we say something often matters just as much as what we say.

Since we're talking about intention, this bears repeating:

The written word is interpreted by the feelings and emotions of the reader, not the intention of the writer.

You might send a message with the best of intentions, but if the person on the other end is having a rough day, they might read it very differently.

Now, I'm not saying you have to switch to all verbal, face-to-face conversations. But you do need to be aware of who you're talking to, how well you know them, and what kind of message you're sending. Sarcasm might land perfectly with someone you know well, and completely miss with someone you don't.

The better your connection with someone, the more likely your words will be received the way you intended. That's true for work, for friendships, for life in general. Connection smooths communication.

Here's an example of where I've had to check myself by thinking about my words' impact. I started writing up an email (oh, key tip… don't put in your recipient until you're done with your email… it'll save you a lot of heartache later…) that was requesting something I needed.

As I took the time to re-read what I had written (Yes, this is an important step), I realized that if you looked at it a certain way, I was coming off as demanding and harsh when that was the farthest from my intention.

I tried a couple times to reword the email, before I gave up, got up from my desk and went over to talk to the person. I decided to avoid even the potential of a bad situation because I was aware that my email could be interpreted badly.

With so much of our communications these days being electronic, it becomes even more important to be careful about not only what we say, but how we say it. And never mind that what you write online lives forever. It's just a good habit to pause and think before responding.

As I said earlier, everything is moving faster, including how quickly misunderstandings can form and how we can hurt each other without even trying. My wife and I taught our children to always try to speak to a person live whenever there's a problem, just as we were taught. We've seen too many friendships end over unresolved issues. Ghosting and deleting friends is now normal… and it hurts.

One of our family mottos is that "the situation is not more important than the relationship". This is how even when we're upset with someone, we use this as our bar to decide how hard to push—or whether it's worth holding our ground. Sometimes it is fine to just agree to disagree if that maintains the relationship.

Some habits from earlier generations, like picking up the phone or showing up in person, still have a place today. Because especially in this digital world we live in, connection and understanding are what really matter.

Chapter 4: Emotional Intelligence and Connection

One of, if not THE biggest factor into how you connect with others—or whether you even feel like you can—is your emotional state. This is where Emotional Intelligence (EQ) comes in.

What is Emotional Intelligence (EQ)? Most people know what IQ is. It's tied to logic, reasoning, and problem-solving—things you can test and score. But EQ often feels more vague, and 'fuzzy.' That's because EQ isn't about standardized tests—it's about how we show up with others, and how we manage ourselves internally.

Here's a simple definition: Emotional intelligence is your ability to understand and manage your own emotions, and to recognize, respond to, and influence the emotions of others.

The five core EQ traits are:

- Self-awareness – Knowing what you feel and why
- Self-regulation – Managing emotional reactions effectively
- Motivation – Channeling emotion toward positive goals
- Empathy – Understanding what others are feeling
- Social skill – Navigating relationships and communication with tact

Why this is so important for us to be aware of is because we are by nature social creatures. We are around people all the time, whether that's in a work group setting or just grabbing some groceries at the local store. It is a quality that helps you to:

1. Maintain our calm and composure when frustration and stress sets in. It helps us to be able to collect ourselves to move past the moment and keep on task.
2. Read the room or individual to know when someone is feeling "off" without needing to even converse with them.

3. Act and react with empathy and attempt to understand before knee jerking to defensiveness and shutting down.
4. Connect with people in a way that makes them feel comfortable not only with you, but also with themselves while they're with you. Let them know that you not only see, but hear them truly.

When Emotional Intelligence gets hard

How you handle all of your relationships is a factor of your emotional intelligence.

Want some great news?

Emotional intelligence, unlike IQ, which tends to stay relatively static, is *learnable*. Through effort and practice, you can improve your abilities to interact with others and be kinder to yourself in the process.

Think of it as a workout for your mind. The more you engage in the "mind gym" the stronger you will get — and the more comfortable and confident you will be with yourself and how you feel in social environments.

So that sounds easy, but much like going to the gym and not knowing which exercise or machine is used for what, it is important to have a workout plan and even better if you have a trainer or coach to help you.

Here are some examples of how people work on building EQ.

Journaling

- Track what triggers your emotional responses—good or bad.
- Lots of people swear by it as a way to take stock of themselves and their day.

- Personally, I've tried it but I'm too inconsistent. That's fine. Just like the gym: the best workout is the one you'll *actually do*.

Practice deeper listening

- If you're like me, you want to jump in with a thought as soon as it hits you.
- Suppressing that urge takes work, but it helps you hear what people really mean.
- Everyday conversations are practice reps—friends, spouse, cashier at the store.
- Slip up? Don't beat yourself up. Even practicing once counts as a workout.

Learning to identify, name, and process emotions

- **Physical cues:** notice your body. Clenched teeth? Racing heart? Those are triggers.
- **First reaction:** do you clam up, walk away, or fire back? Awareness helps.
- **Ask what you're feeling:** don't just ignore a bad mood—try to name it. Naming makes it easier to manage.
- **Write it down:** dump raw emotion onto a page instead of onto someone else. Sometimes I just type it out, feel better, then delete it. Other times it sparks a helpful conversation with my wife.
- **Feel the feels:** allow yourself to have a bad day without judgment. Communicate that to loved ones so they know it's not about them. Then give yourself permission to start fresh tomorrow.

Now, like the gym, you don't have to stick to one workout or exercise.

Start with what you know you'll do, but you may find that in doing that, you're learning on how to do one of the other approaches without even thinking about it.

The single most important thing, like starting an exercise program, is to start! And in the vein of feeling the feels, forgive yourself if you skip or forget. Just start again!

Consistency is how you receive the benefit and build your strength in understanding yourself first and then the people around you.

Now that we've explored what EQ is, and how to build a practice around emotional awareness and regulation, what does that look like in the real world?

What happens when you've done the work, but the people around you aren't responding?

Or worse, when they don't respond at all? This is where emotional intelligence gets tested, and where it starts to shine.

Back to the gym metaphor. What's the hardest thing about working out at the gym? Is it the exercises? The complicated machines? The classes? The trainers? Nope. I think we can all agree that the hardest thing about working out is really, GOING TO THE GYM in the first place. If you go, you generally work out. But there are so many reasons not to go.

What makes you do it?

You want the results of your efforts to pay off so that you can feel healthier physically and, in many cases, mentally too.

So, keeping consistent is hard. Check. What happens to that consistency when you don't see the results you want? It tests your commitment and makes you question what you're doing. However, those who work out will almost invariably tell you that it is important to just keep going. You may not see the results, but things are happening. It is in the process that the rewards show, not the end of the race.

Much like with working out, the hardest part of staying connected isn't the techniques, it's the consistency. Especially when no one replies. This is when your emotional intelligence practice matters most, when the connection feels one-sided, and you're tempted to stop showing up.

One of the strongest EQ practices I've learned, and one that has helped me navigate one-sided connection… is this: assume positive intent.

I try to deal with that by communicating with that same attitude. That's why I always try to lead with positive intent. I don't mean quoting motivational posters. I mean genuinely thinking good thoughts about the person as I write. Even in a short message. Because I believe that energy travels. That mindset carries through. Even in text.

You never know what someone is dealing with. Your message might be the one good moment they have all day. It might make them smile. It might get a reply. It might not. But either way…it mattered.

A New Perspective

Years ago, I was going through a rough stretch at work.

There was another executive I had to collaborate with frequently, and nearly every interaction left me frustrated, annoyed, or worse, furious. Their emails came off as abrupt, dismissive, and to me… very condescending. I started to dread seeing their name pop up in my inbox. I braced myself every time, expecting to feel disrespected or undermined.

And once that story took root in my mind, that this person didn't respect me, it started to color everything.

One day, I was venting to another leader I trusted. I told him how angry I was, how I felt like every message was a slight, how I didn't even want to respond anymore.

He listened patiently and then offered just three words of advice:

"Assume positive intent."

My eyebrows rose. I snorted. "Um... what?"

He repeated himself. I thought he was kidding.

He wasn't.

He told me that if I kept interpreting every message through the lens of hostility, I was the one keeping the conflict alive. Instead, he challenged me to flip the script, to try assuming that this person wasn't being a jerk... they were just under pressure. Or distracted. Or maybe a little bit awkward over email.

At first, I hated that idea. I wanted to be right. I wanted to stay mad.

But I tried it.

And when the next blunt message came in, I paused. I re-read it, but this time with the assumption that they meant well. That they were only trying to get something done. That they weren't trying to insult me; they just weren't sugar-coating it.

Everything changed.

The tone didn't seem as sharp. The urgency made more sense. I could negotiate deadlines more effectively now, because I was no longer reacting out of anger, I was responding with logic.

Did all the stress go away? No. The executive didn't change, but my reaction did. I could now focus on solving the problem, not resenting the person. My own assumptions had made the relationship almost untenable, whereas now it was at least civil.

Eventually that executive left for another company. I had endured their time, but came out of it with a lesson that I've applied to my life ever since.

That's the power of assuming positive intent. It doesn't just change how you read a message; it changes how you feel about people. It allows you to keep connecting, without carrying the emotional baggage of imagined conflict.

Now, I'm not saying you should assume positive intent when it's *obvious* the message isn't coming from a good place. Sometimes people just aren't kind. But most of the time, you can't be 100% sure in the moment. So unless it's glaring, it's better to lean toward positive intent. Worst case, you stay calm and professional. Best case, you dodge a conflict that never needed to happen.

Much like giving a gift, connection is about offering something with no guaranteed return. So make sure that what you're offering… your words, your attention, your check-ins all come from a good place.

Chapter 5: Connection in Times of Change

It's easy to stay consistent when things are going well. But the one constant in life (no, not death and taxes) is change. It could be a life-altering moment—or just one of those days where you have more meetings than minutes.

Change knocks us out of our rhythm. It makes us pull back. We cancel plans, ignore texts, put connection on the back burner. And sometimes, that's necessary. We need rest. We need solitude. But those moments of disruption are also when connection can matter most.

Here's a story of how that happened to me. I certainly wasn't expecting it—and it truly made all the difference.

The Friend I Didn't Know I Had

I remember when I got laid off back in 2023. This was a completely new experience to me since I had survived dozens of layoffs from several companies. I had never really done much job searching because I always found new opportunities through people. However, it didn't work out that way after being laid off.

One thing I did immediately was to start working my way through my network, especially the ones that had the most power and influence, to see what opportunities I might be able to develop with their help.

Most were sympathetic, but unfortunately not in a position to bring me on. I reached out to other folks I've known for a long time, and frankly got a lot of unsatisfying responses such as "It'll all work out," or "You'll find something." Honestly, saying nothing would have been better than hearing that.

There were definitely some of my connections that helped me a lot—providing suggestions, sending job postings, checking in—and

I appreciate them as much today as I did then. But I want to bring up a specific connection.

I reached out to a gentleman that I had recently worked with before I got laid off. His company had been assisting ours, and we had developed a good rapport over the last couple of years. I knew Jacob professionally, but not all that well personally.

When I told him of my situation, he immediately offered his support and put in actual effort to help me. He checked in his company, made calls to people in my area, and really went beyond anything I would have expected from someone I only knew as a work acquaintance.

He barely knew me, but he knew my work ethic and personality, and he continued to stay in touch, provide options, and heartfelt support.

Eventually, I ended up setting up a consulting company since the job search was going nowhere. Not long after, Jacob left his company and formed one of his own.

I mentioned that if he ever needed support, I'd be glad to help him since I was already familiar with his business, having been on the receiving end.

He took me up on that offer.

Without the work that I was able to get helping him, I don't see how my family could have survived. My whole life, and that of my family, was impacted because he responded when I needed it most.

Of course, change doesn't always happen to us. Sometimes we're just there when it's happening to someone else. And sometimes, you build a connection through the change—without even realizing how important it's going to become.

Peace in a Time of Crisis

The pandemic was, in many ways, the biggest change that anyone had seen in a lifetime. We went from a 21st century fast pace to everything slowing down.

We were all stuck in place, disconnected from our normal routines, waiting for life to start again. But even then, especially then, connection was still possible.

Here's a story about one of the most unexpected and valuable connections I made during that time.

March 2020. We'd been told to grab all of our stuff from work and to work from home until notified otherwise. The pandemic had begun. I was one of the fortunate people who was still able to work full-time and not really have my job affected by the shift. But the transition from a place where I experienced a high degree of live social interaction to being at home where all my work connections were digital and very planned… that was rough.

That's when I saw a communication on Slack about some people offering yoga classes over video a couple times a week. One had her times early in the morning, while the other had hers right at lunchtime. I'd never really practiced yoga, but it was something I had always wanted to try. I made the decision to join the noon class—and that's when I met Kat.

Kat worked in a completely different area of the company that I had no real interaction with. Additionally, her office was in another state from the home office. We had never met before this. I took the first class, and then another, and another. I was very grateful for being able to turn the screen off and mute so that no one could see my terrible form or hear me grunting from trying to stretch my body in ways I hadn't before.

My favorite part of the sessions was the end pose called savasana. It seems simple, but it actually isn't. The idea is that you are perfectly still—not just your body (and believe me, that's hard enough), but also calming your mind. It's a pose of simply being. And in our world today, being still feels like we should be doing something.

When I first started taking yoga, there were several of us. Then the numbers dropped to where I wasn't just a visitor—I was one of the regulars. I kept up the practice through the entire pandemic, and found a great deal of peace, which helped me through it all and connect better with the most important person... myself.

By now Kat and I were work friends. We'd chat a little bit about work things and such, but mostly just about yoga. Then, she decided to enter a bodybuilding competition. That may sound surprising, but Kat is a dancer, performer, weightlifter, and yogi. She placed very high in her first competition and actually started training other people in weightlifting.

I've been weightlifting most of my life, but could see the benefit of a trainer, and so I hired Kat.

Fast forward to now—Kat is a person I reach out to with struggles and concerns, and one who I support in turn. It's been five years since we met online to do yoga, and to this day... we still HAVE NOT MET.

Connection is not limited by time or distance. If I can have a good friend I've never met in person, then you can find connection in your life too.

Kat clearly showed me that you don't need to be in the same space to share support. Jacob reminded me that even newer connections can become lifelines when it counts.

Those moments, whether sparked by crisis or curiosity, don't just help us ride out the change. They help us anchor to something deeper: to friendships, to meaning, to each other.

Change is a constant. That's a guarantee. And while it may tempt us to shut down or pull inward, it's also a powerful invitation to reach out. To connect.

Because connection isn't just something we do when life is easy. It's something we lean on when everything else gets hard.

So even when change pushes you to retreat…
Show up. Be real. Stay open.

That's how connection can find a way… right through the heart of change.

Section II: Building the Habit

Keeping connections and staying in touch doesn't just happen. It's a process—one that starts with small actions and builds over time. In this section, we'll look at what it takes to create that kind of consistency, along with some pointers to help you start your own journey in a way that feels natural and comfortable to you.

Chapter 6: Building Habits Around Staying in Touch

Now that we're thinking about connection, how do we turn it into a habit?

I'd love to give you an inspiring story—one of those moments where lightning struck, angels sang, and it all suddenly made sense. But I'm afraid I can't.

For me, it built up slowly, over time — starting in high school (we'll get to that later), continuing through my early work years, and deepening in my <ahem> later ones. If there was a turning point, it was probably when I accepted that I genuinely enjoy making people smile and laugh. Not in a stand-up comedian way, more in the friendly, neighborly sense.

As I learned to accept myself more fully, I started noticing something: I always felt better after talking to people.

Any people.

Not just close friends or coworkers… anyone.

No grand speeches. No dramatic scenes. Just small moments of connection in everyday life.

And at some point, it stopped being something I meant to do.
It became something I just did.
Eventually, it became part of who I am.

Now, I know what you might be thinking:
"That's great for you, Marc… but I don't have 40 years to spare."

Don't worry.

What I've learned along the way is exactly what I want to share with you, so that however much you want to improve (and that's completely up to you), you'll have ideas and tools that make it easier to start.

First things first: this should be obvious, but I'm going to say it anyway.

Habits… good or bad… take time.
Building a connection habit is no different.

Here's the good news: if you're just looking for quick, low-effort ways to stay in touch with people, this book has you covered. I've got tooltips and strategies to help you do that without adding stress to your life.

But if you're looking to connect more deeply and in more meaningful, satisfying ways…
That's going to take some conscious effort.

Will the payoff be worth it? Only you can answer that.

But in my experience, a life spent enjoying time with your fellow humans is a pretty cool one.

The World We're Connecting In

Before we dive into how to build the habit, let's take a quick look at the environment we're building it in.

Connection today isn't the same as it was for our parents—or even for us a few decades ago. The tools have changed. The pace has changed. And so have the expectations.

As a parent of two adult children, it's been fascinating to watch how the social dynamic has shifted with phones and social media. What's struck me most is this: everything that happened in my youth—

good, bad, and awkward—still happens today. The core drivers haven't changed. People still want to feel seen, liked—included. We're still chasing belonging, popularity, purpose—just like we always have.

But now? It all happens super-fast.

I'm not saying that's good or bad. Just different. What's really changed is how people respond when they're upset, disappointed, or feeling disconnected.

I was raised to work things out face-to-face. If there was an issue with someone, you found them and talked it through. And if you couldn't do that, you picked up the phone.

That mattered—because face-to-face gives you so much context. You can read body language, see expressions, hear tone. Even on a phone call, you still get emotional cues: the pace, the pauses, the inflection. How someone says something can be just as important as what they say.

Of course, those were the only tools we had.

Today? Phones changed the entire dynamic. These are the super-powered, handheld computer-children of their old rotary analog parents. And the "phone" part? That's often the least-used feature.

Texting, Snapchat, Facebook, TikTok—these are now the dominant ways people connect. And again, that's not inherently bad. A tool is just a tool. It all depends on how you use it.

Now, I'm not saying you have to use any of these tools. But if you want to connect with someone, it's really helpful to understand how they prefer to communicate—regardless of your personal preferences.

The funny thing is, people don't just connect differently across generations—they connect differently even within the same family. My kids had two grandmothers who couldn't have been more different in how they reached out, and how that shaped their relationships.

A Story of Two Grandmothers

My kids had two grandmothers, both of whom lived in different states from us.

My wife's mom took a more traditional approach: she didn't reach out to her children unless they called her. She expected them to initiate. She rarely emailed, and absolutely refused to text. I'm pretty sure she was still using AOL until the day she passed.

My mom, on the other hand, wasn't a tech wizard—but she embraced electronic communication. We'd schedule video calls. She texts and emails regularly. She figured out what worked not just for her kids, but for her grandkids, too.

So where am I going with this?

My mother-in-law often complained that she didn't talk to the grandkids very much. And we gently explained, "They respond to texts. That's just how they connect."

She didn't want to adapt.

And as a result, her relationship with them stayed more distant.

My mom? She talks to me all the time—and when she wants to reach the kids, she texts them. Simple as that. Because of that, they know her better. She's present in their world in a way that feels natural to them.

The difference came down to one simple thing:
My mom met them where they were.

My mother-in-law didn't. And that made all the difference.

Bonus Tip: This Works Both Ways

Want to make your parents' day?

Send them a note in the mail.
A card. Just because.

(Double bonus points if you write it in cursive. 😊)

Where the rubber meets the road

So what does it take to be good at connecting?

Honestly, it pretty much starts and ends with the will to do so. If you truly don't want to connect with people, then you're not going to get any good at it.

Think of school. You probably did really well in classes you actually liked. And in the ones you didn't? Maybe you scraped by, or maybe you got a decent grade but didn't retain much afterward. Same with connection. If you're not genuinely interested, it won't stick.

But sometimes, you have to commit before you're convinced.

Let's take the gym, for example (yes, I use gym metaphors a lot).

When you first start going, it's tough. Your body isn't used to the movements. You feel sore, awkward, maybe even defeated. It feels like torture just to get there… so you can continue torturing yourself in new ways, in different parts of your body.

That's how a lot of people feel about starting (or restarting) connection habits.

But fast forward a year: the pain of going is replaced by the discomfort of not going. You actually start to like the soreness, because it means you're making progress. You pushed through. You stayed consistent. And suddenly, something you once dreaded has become something you crave.

That's what I'm saying here.

Connection might feel like a chore at first. That's fair.
But give it a real shot. Give it time.
Stick with it for a year.

If you still don't like it, at least you gave it your best shot.
But I'd bet that it'll surprise you. It may become something you enjoy.
And more than that—it'll become part of who you are.

Let's tackle the hardest part of building any habit… Starting.

> **Toolkit: Starter Moves To Build That (Connection) Workout Habit**

If we stick with the gym theme, most trainers will tell you the same thing when you're just starting out: take it slow.

Light weights, don't overdo it, let your body get used to the movements.

So that's what we're going to do here. If you're ready to start building your connection habit, but aren't sure what that actually looks like, here are a few easy, doable ideas to get you going. Think of them like light reps.

These aren't meant to overwhelm you. Just small things you can do. Consistently.

Low-Effort Starters (Warm-ups)

- Send one "Hey, was thinking about you" text per day (or week if that's too much).
- Keep a running list of "people I like" in your Notes app. When someone crosses your mind, add them. This becomes your go-to roster for check-ins.
- At the end of meetings or casual conversations, thank someone by name (Remember to smile!).

Medium-Energy Builders (Form Work)

- Set one calendar reminder per week labeled "Reach Out." No guilt... simply a nudge.
- Comment meaningfully on a friend's post, not just a like. Let them feel seen.
- Start your own mini-coffee club: one person per month. (Virtual counts too!)

Deeper Connection Moves (Heavy Lifts)

- Write someone a real letter or card. Doesn't have to be long, it's the effort and the gesture alone that stands out.
- Pick someone you've drifted from... and own the drift. "Hey, I know it's been a while. Would love to catch up." You'd be surprised how often people are happy to hear from you.
- Ask better questions. Instead of "How's work?" try "What's been challenging you lately?" or "What's bringing you joy right now?"

Remember, this isn't about impressing anyone, or worse, checking a "to-do" box. It's about showing up in simple, human ways, consistently. How you choose to do your reaching out is up to you and what tools you're comfortable with. Which is why we're talking about that next.

Chapter 7: Tools of the Trade – Phones, Calendars, & Contact Lists

Ok, so now that we're going to start building this habit of connection, how are we going to do it?

The Phone: Your Swiss Army Knife

Let's start with the obvious: your phone is your single most powerful connection device. Texting, video chats, messaging apps, emails…this hand-held computer does it all. And yes, believe it or not, you can still use it to actually call people.

Our phones are always with us, always on, and packed with features we often overlook. Most people think of phones as communication tools, but they're also **connection systems**. With just a few changes, your phone can go from something that distracts you to something that reminds you who you care about and why.

Call or Voicemail? Don't Overthink It

Let's start with talking. For a lot of folks, this is the least attractive option because if you have to leave a message you don't want to sound all babbling and all over the place. (Believe me, I've left my share of those).

But let's take it with the two options:

> **Call goes through:**
> You actually reach the person you were reaching out to! A couple things you should work on doing (and I constantly need to remind myself).
>
> - **Ask if this is a good time to talk.** Some people will always answer their phone even at inopportune times for

them. By asking, you give them the ability to gracefully exit if they need to. This may also give them the opportunity to say how much time they have.
- **Use their time wisely** - If they have time, then you're good to go with any conversation you wish. If not, then depending on what you want to chat about, it is best to use the moment to find another time that is convenient to them

Call goes to voicemail – Ah... the dreaded voicemail... what do I say now?

- **Voicemail setup** - Hopefully their voicemail is set up. You wouldn't believe how many people have had their phones for years and never set up their voicemail. (Hint: If you haven't, consider rectifying that ☺)
- **Keep it short** – Voicemails have limited time so anything you say should be short and sweet. I've noticed that my check-ins when leaving a message are normally around a one-minute to one and a half-minute maximum time.
- **Use a script** – Practice if you need to. Write out what you want to say, and go over it until it comes out naturally.
- **Relax** – Most voicemail systems let you delete or re-record. You're safe! Keep changing it until you hit your stride.

Texting: Most Used, Least Leveraged

Without question, texting is the undisputed champion as the preferred method of communication, particularly in regular day-to-day settings. It's direct, to the point, and a great way to send a message without interrupting the person receiving it.

So, if it's the most used, then why isn't it the king (or queen) of connection? Well... it is, and it isn't. People tend to text folks in their immediate circles all the time, but rarely beyond that. It's become so routine that we forget it can still be a powerful way to reach across great distances instantly.

I'm encouraging you to use this tool to build and sustain relationships that are important to you, even if they're inconvenient, whether due to time or geography.

I know people across the country and the world, so when I think about texting, I try to keep things like time zones in mind—especially around response expectations. A good way to think about this is through growing concentric circles:

Small Circle
This is probably that 50-mile radius or so. Why 50? Because it's still a workable driving distance if you want to meet in person. In this range, I'm checking in, but I also have the option to set up a live conversation, grab a coffee, or meet up to build the relationship further.

Medium Circle
Now we're starting to spread out into other states and time zones. Unless someone is traveling and happens to be in your area, a live meetup is unlikely. This is where most people tend to fall off... and also where the greatest opportunity lives.

The first step here is to push past that natural "out of sight, out of mind" tendency. I reach out to a lot of folks in this space. Some answer, some don't, but I don't want to lose touch just because I didn't try. There are plenty of great ways to gather with people virtually, but more often than not, it starts with a text.

Large Circle

These are the truly long-distance connections. When I send a message to someone in London, for example, I have to think about what time it is over there. If I send something out at a time convenient for me, I might not get a response until the next day. But that's okay. I don't reach out every day, or even every month, but eventually, I circle back. It's a good feeling to know you've got friends in far-off places.

Your Hidden Goldmine: Contact Lists

Having trouble remembering who you'd even like to connect with? That's not unusual, in fact, I'd bet it's one of the biggest reasons people don't reach out more often. Life is busy, we have to keep track of work, shopping, bills, kids, you name it. Sometimes it is tough to just remember which day it is.

To combat this, I give you <cue fanfare>... contact lists. Oh, I know you have them. Our phones are filled with them; social media is chock full of them.

Ok, maybe now you're thinking, great, I went from not knowing who to reach out to, to having more people to sort through than I know what to do with. Thanks for the informational avalanche, Marc...

First of all, I'm not saying you need to form strong connections with EVERYONE. That alone would take more time in a day than any of us have. So just on that, your list will cut down considerably.

Here are some ways that I've found how to mine these veins of contact data to help fuel my own habits. Perhaps they'll be helpful to you.

Phone Contacts

I'll be completely honest when I tell you that I've probably only been utilizing this in the last five years or so, but this is how it started. You know how around the holidays, say Thanksgiving, you may call or text family to wish them well? I remember vividly the day I took that to a new level.

Happy Textgiving

Picture the scene. The room around the kitchen is warm and filled with the aroma of delicious food that the family patiently waited for to dig into their holiday feast.

If you're not immediately helping with dinner, what is there to do? That year I really wasn't into watching football (Sorry Dallas and Detroit), or anything on the television. Like many folks, I picked up my phone. By this time, I'd already wished my family Happy Thanksgiving, and expected to talk to them on the phone later that day. Since it was a day of thanks, I clicked over to my contact list and started at "A". I located a number of people that I wanted to wish well, so I did. Then I went to "B", and you get the idea.

By the time I was done, I had texted out Happy Thanksgiving wishes to well over 60 people. It didn't feel weird, it felt good. People were touched. Several even asked how I was doing. And just like that, a bunch of meaningful check-ins happened while the turkey was still in the oven.

That's when I knew I hit on something.

And here's the real point: your phone contacts aren't just names. They're opportunities waiting for a spark — and all it takes is a moment to turn a list into a connection.

Every now and then, I go through my contact list on my phone. Maybe I start at A, perhaps S.

It doesn't matter where you start.

I'll scan through and find a few folks that I've not talked to in a while and shoot them off a text. Nothing too lengthy or difficult. Mostly it is something like "Hey. Just reaching out to drop a line. Hope you're well".

It ensures that I still keep in touch with people I know and it isn't overwhelming.

I'd be willing to bet that every one of you has someone that can probably say "Wow, it's been a while since I talked to them", is sitting there on your phone, waiting.

Social Media Contact Lists
Ok, this is the informational overload mentioned earlier. Facebook, LinkedIn ... pick a platform, anyone even remotely active will acquire hundreds of "friends" or acquaintances over a relatively short period of time.

Now you could be asking, "Marc, do you seriously go through all of your LinkedIn contacts?". It's a good question and the answer is no. I do however tend to roll through my contacts on LinkedIn (what I use most) to see if I need to remove very light connections, etc. In the course of doing that, I end up seeing names of people I've worked with and that in turn spurs my action to sending a LinkedIn message.

I'm not on all of the platforms so I certainly can't provide specifics on how to approach this for them, but what I can do is tell you that the basic concept is the same.

Take a few moments to review who you have on your lists. It's ok if you remove people, sometimes relationships simply go in different directions. Whether you do or don't isn't the point. It is about taking a look over your lists and seeing if there are any relationships you'd like to build, strengthen or maybe even repair.

One thing to be clear on here is that response times can vary drastically on social media depending on the person, and frankly, the generation.

I've noticed that on LinkedIn, if you're perfectly happy in your day to day working life and career, or not actively using it to network, that people *might* pop on once a month…maybe. I've had people respond to me as much as six months after I reached out because they just didn't go onto the app.

On the other hand, as I've noticed by observing my daughter, there are some people that ONLY respond via social media messaging even over their phone texts.

The only way to find out is to reach out, but remember to be patient as you really don't know how people utilize these various apps in their lives.

Contact lists… who knew?

This is a gold mine. Happy digging!

Calendar & Reminders: Building Rhythms That Stick

Calendars? Really? But I use my calendar all the time … in fact it feels like my calendar runs me!

All valid, but they're missing one key ingredient. Most people's calendars are set for events, not as a tool to build or maintain connection. Now I said *most* - because I know plenty of people do use calendars for social stuff. My wife, for example, regularly schedules check-ins with friends in other states. So, I know they are used. What I'm talking about is to tweak your thinking on calendars and how they can be an invaluable tool to help you build a habit... if that's what you're aiming for.

Let's look at two types:

Physical Calendars

I know, this may sound outdated. Most people use digital tools now. But there's something about a paper calendar that we tend to overlook.

You see, a physical calendar always shows you the entire month. The full month's right there—no clicks, no tabs, no swiping. Just a clean, visible reminder of what's coming up. That makes it perfect for planning, not only meetings, but moments of connection.

How can it be a useful connection tool? Let's think, when using electronic calendars, you generally are looking at a week at a time at most. Even if you look at a month, everything can become a blur of colored meetings. Whereas when you look at that calendar in your office, it's big, you can write things clearly on it, and you look at it EVERY DAY.

Hey, guess what that is? A habit you already have and don't even need to work on! So, now all we need to do is write down the days and times that we want to reach out. The fact that we see it every day will reinforce it as something that you want to do.

When you take that, combine it with your digital calendar and throw on reminders. Now you're really cooking with gas (that means you're doing well for all of you not from New England.).

Digital Calendars & Reminders

There's more types than I care to count or name. Chances are, you're probably using one as part of your everyday life and not even thinking about it. What I love about these are that they are the ultimate in portable. They live on your phone, your laptop, anywhere you are, and you can access your calendar with relative ease. The question though, is do you use them as ways to build a habit to reach out to people, or does that mainly stay relegated to birthdays and anniversaries?

If that sounds like you, don't worry. I think that literally is most of us. I bring these tools up as options of how you can use things in your regular life to help you find the time and ways of bringing the thoughts of connection to the forefront and not so "out of sight".

If you have trouble remembering to reach out, why not try a calendar entry? Even better, add a reminder with a sound or something to really get your attention. These tools that we already carry and use every day? They make this so easy. Again, it's up to you if you want to utilize this method.

Now understand that even if you put it on a calendar, that doesn't mean you'll do it.

I get it.

Life gets nuts, things happen.

However, I do guarantee this. If you have it on a calendar, and especially with a reminder, you WILL see it. Which means that the choice of action will be yours. If you don't have a way to bring your attention to it, then you'll find that days or weeks go by before you remember —wait, I was going to reach out to someone.

What if you just don't have the time? Reschedule it! It takes almost no time to do and then you can get back to what needs doing.

No guilt. Simply time management.

So, if we want to change that, to get out more and connect more, we'll need a different rhythm. One we can stick with.

> Toolkit: Tools of the Trade

What you use for your tools and how you choose who to reach out to is completely up to you. Here are some quick guides under each option:

Tools to Work

- Alphabet scrolling helps you pick a person to reach out to
- Set reminders for catching up with specific people
- Use your time – Waiting at the doctors, car drives, etc.

Tools of the Trade – Using Them Well

Phone Calls

- Keep voicemails under a minute.
- When calling, check if they have time to talk.

Texting

- Use short, genuine check-ins (*"Thinking of you"* works wonders).
- Skip sarcasm/jokes unless you're sure they'll land.

Social Media

- Use direct messages for real connection.
- Be patient with responses—different platforms move at different speeds.

Chapter 8: Consistency Is King (or Queen)

Building consistency isn't about doing one big thing. It's about staying on top of small things, and doing them again... and again. Sounds obvious. Well, it is. But I've noticed in life that just because something is simple, doesn't mean it is easy. Consistency meets that definition to a tee.

In fact, most books on improvement talk about making small changes to your habits and gradually incorporating them into your life. These small alterations lead to big changes over time.

Let's face it, you don't have to overhaul your life or become a professional "connector." You only need to find something you'll actually do on a regular basis.

As I've said before: do the exercise you'll actually do. That same principle applies here. If texting one person a week feels doable, start there. If walking into a room and saying hi to someone new at work once a day feels right, go with that.

You don't need to go from 1 to 100 miles per hour overnight. You need to find and pick a speed that keeps you moving.

So, how do you actually start building consistency?

Simple: Start Small.

> **Toolkit: Building Your Consistent Workout**

Just like lifting weights, doing too much too soon doesn't feel right—and worse, you risk getting hurt. Start light and build up as your strength improves. It's the same with connection.

Of course, you have to pick a place to start. This will vary depending on your personality and current comfort level with social interaction. But here are some ways to start, and stay on track.

Determine who you want to connect more with.

- A friend or family member you've drifted from?
- A new acquaintance you want to build a relationship with?
- A colleague you'd like to know better?
- A potential mentor you admire?

Find a cadence that feels doable.

- Start slow. Two check-ins over a month may feel like nothing—but it's something. And something is better than nothing.
- Remember: it's not about volume, it's about showing up.

Use tools to help.

- Set reminders on your phone.
- Write it on a calendar you look at regularly.
- Use sticky notes: "Remember to call Bill next Thursday."

Figure out when and where you're most comfortable reaching out.

- Are you a morning person with energy before the day kicks in?
- Do you prefer chatting at home, from your office, or even from the car?
- Can you multitask—call someone while walking or driving?

Here's an example of where just having a quick conversation with someone led to something unexpected and wonderful.

The Professor in the Lobby

I was in Austin during an event called Startup Week—a convention where new startup founders and owners gathered to exchange ideas and attend workshops on funding, networking, and more. I was there mostly for business development of my own business, so I naturally gravitated toward the more crowded areas to get contacts and potential prospects.

While in the lobby, I noticed a well-dressed woman accompanied by about seven equally sharp college-aged women. They were clearly together, and as they approached, I made eye contact, smiled, and said hello. I introduced myself and asked, half-jokingly, why she had an "entourage." She laughed and introduced herself as Kelly, a professor of entrepreneurship at a Texas university. She was there with her students to give them real-world exposure to how startups navigate challenges like funding and networking.

When I told her I did fractional CFO consulting, her eyes lit up with interest. She asked if I'd be possibly interested in doing a Zoom seminar for her class on financial topics. I said sure, and we exchanged contact info before parting.

A few days later, I followed up with Kelly by email. She responded enthusiastically, and after a bit of back-and-forth, we settled on a topic: real-world financial literacy for life after college. The session, titled 'Things You Should Be Aware of and Prepare For... After School,' was held as a video meeting in February 2024. It was a subject that I could really get into as I had literally worked with my daughter on this very subject when discussing if she was really financially able to move out. This added a very real element to the talk. When the call ended, I wasn't sure how it landed—but Kelly told me afterward that her students, even though they were quiet during the session, did enjoy it and appreciated the real talk.

I've now done that same talk for several times. It's become a real high point of my year. The last couple of times, I've even traveled to campus to speak in person—and doing it live is a completely different (and better) experience. Now I genuinely look forward to when Kelly reaches out each semester to coordinate the next date.

All of this—this ongoing, rewarding experience—started with a simple hello. Think about that. That's the power of connection. You never know what it might grow into.

Now, not all of your connections are going to blossom that well or that quickly. Most of my connections personally are ones that are just built up by random check ins, annual good wishes on birthdays, holidays, etc. A good example of one of those connections is my friend Chris.

Role Playing and Hair Metal Bands

We actually met through one of my younger brothers since Chris was in his class. We developed a strong bond of our love of playing Dungeons and Dragons and 80s hair bands. In fact, we were roommates for first year I moved out of my parent's house. Then, inevitably, things changed. I moved across the country, got married, had kids, and we lost touch for probably a good 10 years.

At this point, most people go their separate ways and pretty much that's that. I added Chris to my check ins on Thanksgiving and Christmas, but I think what was the most consistent and fun was our check ins based only on music.

How did that work? I had to drive a lot for work and I would invariably listen to music at some point. When a hair band would come on, that would bring me back to that time of my life when Chris and I hung out more. I would then take a picture of the song playing in the car (yes, when stopped), and text it to him. It usually brought a "LOL" or something like that, but then he started doing it to me as well.

We did that for years. Every now and again we would talk on the phone, but it was mostly the silly hair band pics that we stayed connected with.

Today I've reconnected strongly with Chris and we talk all the time. It's like no time has passed at all. He's been a big supporter for me to write not only this book, but some other ideas I've had over time.

All of your connections don't have to be super deep to be powerful. Just a little check-in now and then—even once a year—can keep a relationship alive.

And sometimes, like with Chris, those light-touch moments become the thread that holds it all together until one day, without much fanfare, you're back in each other's lives like no time has passed.

Consistency doesn't have to mean rigid schedules or forced effort. It can start as a simple impulse—a photo, a song, a laugh—and grow from there. Over time, those small moments add up. And before long, you're not just someone who reaches out…

You're someone who can be counted on.

So, how do you get started doing that? Fantastic question, because the next chapter is all about finding connections in ordinary and everyday places.

Chapter 9: Don't Waste the Wait

Part 1: Places You Already Go

We've talked about how consistency is the key. But how do you actually stay consistent? I hear this all the time, "You're good at keeping up with people, but I just don't have time to connect". And there it is. Everyone's reason, excuse, whatever you want to call it. No one feels that they have time. I think you do, but you're likely not seeing the moments as opportunities.

Unless you're holed up all day every day at home, it is a strong bet that you go out at some point. Could be the gym, to get groceries, the commute to work, and so on. All these locations give you time to be able to connect. It's not even really an active effort because you were going to do it anyway. (Ok, I admit, the gym sometimes takes a very active effort, but let's not get sidetracked). Now you could be saying, "HA, I don't like to talk to people at the gym, I'm focused on my workout". That's fair. That means the gym isn't a place where you like to connect. However, it does not mean that there aren't others. In fact, it is in the places where you have to wait that you have the most opportunity.

Think about it.

In the car – If you have a 10-minute commute or 30-minute one, you have choices. I used to have a one-hour commute to work one way. You either find something to do with that time, or you start building a nice pot of road rage. So, what can you do?

You could:

- Listen to music
- Listen to podcasts/audible books
- **Make some calls?**

Of course, doing them hands free in the car is the right way to do it. If you don't have that capability, then the car is not the right spot for you. But if you do, you can leave texts or voicemails to quite a few people before you even get to work! Most of my check-ins are literally about a minute long. And sometimes... sometimes, you actually get the person you're reaching out to. Have you ever been in a good conversation on a long drive and wondered where the time went? That's the teleporting effect of connection!

In the gym – Interactions

- **The front desk** – a cheerful smile and a hello is a great way to help someone else's day as well as yourself.
- **Spot someone** – This is situational, but if someone needs help, be that person. You may make a new contact, you may not, but I know one thing. Even if you don't really talk, that person will remember you next time you're in the gym.
- **Treadmill** – This is hit or miss. If you come with someone, then this is easy, if not, I find most people zone out with headphones.
- **Entering and leaving** – I always seem to be holding the door for someone on the way in and out. Be cheerful and kind. Connection is not always words.

At the store (grocery, department, etc.)

- **Compliment someone** – You may notice someone has a great pair of shoes, a nice outfit, a cool T-shirt. When you're out and about, there are lots of opportunities for you to reach out to someone and make them feel good. And when you do that, you'll love how you feel afterwards too!
- **In line at the grocery store** – This is a great spot for compliments and general conversation. (Yes, the "How about this weather" still works!). I compliment people on well behaved children, or sometimes make comments about the food going on the conveyor belt after mine. That's the "Hmmm, can I come over to your house?" type of moment.

Sometimes it is saying "You doing alright today?" to the cashier.
- **At the store** – If you're in line, you can complement someone's purchase. Talk about the weather. Smile and say hello.

There doesn't need to be a particular "line" for every situation or location. Most of the time it is simply the act of making eye contact, smiling and/or nodding. Conversation can flow from there.

Before we go on with everything being rosy and awesome, understand that sometimes, you may want to talk to folks and are in a great mood, and they are not. You may just get someone staring blankly at you, or turn away – I've seen them all. In those moments I take a line from comedians when they're having a hard time. I call it "a tough room". There's no telling how the "room" is going to be when you go out, but take time to read the moment. You'll know quickly if it is a tough room or not.

But sometimes, it's not the place… it's the moment. Let's look at the slivers of time we often overlook.

Part 2: Time You Didn't Know You Had

So far, we've talked about the places where you already are. Now let's talk about the moments you already live through—those in-between slivers of time that are just sitting there, waiting to be used.

You probably have more spare moments than you realize. Regardless of where you are, at some point you're going to be waiting—whether in a doctor's office or in line at airport security. Waiting is still part of life. (And if you're a Tom Petty fan, it is in fact… "the hardest part.")

So, what do you do while you're waiting. Well, if you're most people these days, you pull out your phone and stare at news, games, whatever. Pay attention here. Doing this even a little less will give you time you didn't know you had.

Waiting

Let's use the doctor's office as an example. I mean, come on… have you ever *not* waited for a doctor? If so, I bet it was the exception, not the rule.

Now, if you're sick, it's probably not the time for connection. But if it's only a check-up, bloodwork, or something minor, you've got an opportunity.

Here's what happened to me the other day:

Fun Where You Find It

I needed to get some standard bloodwork done. The line to check in was long. I smiled at the person in front of me—and at an adorable two-year-old who was busy charming everyone nearby."

No one was particularly chatty, so when I got to the counter, I decided to liven it up. I said: "I'm here for my bloodletting."
The receptionist chuckled. So did the one next to her. Even someone in the line beside me laughed. I followed up with: "Hey, you gotta have fun."

And you know what? They appreciated it. Especially in a doctor's office—where most of the interactions aren't exactly fun. Sometimes those are the best places to bring a little light. These folks deal with a lot of unpleasant stuff. Be a warm glow for them.

You have choices. It could have been a dull 10–15-minute wait, and sometimes you do just want that quiet time. But life is a lot more enjoyable when you don't waste the wait—when you decide to have fun and connect. At least I think so.

Long lines

Ever traveled by air over a holiday? Then you know the drill: you're going to be in a long security line.

Here's the choice you face:

- Be cranky (which doesn't help).
- Or have some fun and make the time pass faster.

I usually choose the second. About 75% of the time, I'll strike up a conversation with the person in front or behind me. The opener is easy: "Where are you off to today?"

Thanks to that one question, I've met:

- People from my hometown.
- Folks from places I used to live.
- Travelers headed somewhere I'd love to go.

It doesn't make the line move faster—but it makes the wait feel lighter.

Between meetings

This one is a bit more work centric, but useful.

Have you ever HAD to get like five minutes with someone and their schedule is rock solid full? I've had this happen all the time. So, I decided to use my time to find ways to get them between events.

Bridging the Between

At my last company, we had a kitchen area and around that was a lounge of sorts with couches. Close by were the restrooms. (I realize not all offices are this well planned and stocked, but the method here can be modified). I used to go and work on one of those couches and basically stake out the area because of these reasons:

Sooner or later, between meetings people would have to go to the restroom;

or

Get something to eat or drink.

I could only do this when I wasn't in meetings, but you get the idea. My stakeout plan worked well: I'd catch people on their way out of the restroom (*do not follow them to it*) or from the kitchen, and get what I needed during the walk. That saved me from trying to wedge into their packed schedules.

What I didn't expect was that it would flip. Soon, colleagues started coming to me for quick questions. What began as a time-saver became a trust-builder.

The Doctor Is In

The questions didn't start right away, but as I started to occupy the same area more consistently, people picked up on something. They knew where to find me. My good stakeout spot turned into my office away from my cube.

Soon, the tech folks would actively seek me out. "Hey, do you have a quick moment?" became a regular refrain. At times I thought about hanging a sign: The doctor is in. And far from being a nuisance, it thrilled me. I loved being someone they could count on. That kind of presence is what real partnership looks like.

What started out as a simple strategy to catch people between meetings ended up opening greater communication, leading to deepening trust and strong connection with my IT coworkers.

Parking Lot Brief

I employed a similar stakeout strategy at another company, but with a twist. My manager always left at the same time each day to pick up her daughter—which made her ultra predictable (which was awesome).

I knew exactly when she'd be free of meetings and calls. So whenever I had something important to discuss, I'd "just happen" to be by her office as she was packing up. Then I'd walk with her on the way out to her car. She wasn't inconvenienced, and I got the conversation and direction I needed.

Remember, this functions in a work environment, but can be creepy outside of it. Don't stake out people outside of the office 😊

These strategies worked for me, but not every idea fits every environment. The good news? Some of the best opportunities show up in the simplest places.

Whether it is a coffee nook, break area, kitchen or snack spot, the "water cooler" conversations of old still happen. These are places where you can make connections with people you'd not usually get to be around. I recall talking at length with the president of the company while I was getting espresso. There are opportunities here for you to get to know people and more importantly, for them to get to know you.

Connection doesn't always need planning; it just needs awareness. These little in-between moments? That's where your habits are built, one small choice at a time.

And sometimes, it's not about timing at all—it's about being open to the world around you.

Part 3: When Curiosity Leads to Connection

When my wife and I moved to Texas, it was a leap of faith. We didn't know many people, and for a good week and a half, our belongings were still in transit. That meant empty rooms, sleeping on air mattresses, and a whole lot of takeout.

Bluegrass Buddies

Thankfully, my wife started hunting for local events to help us get our bearings. Turns out, there was a bluegrass festival happening less than a mile from our house.

Now, neither of us grew up on bluegrass, but being the adventurers we are, we figured ... why not? We grabbed a couple of folding chairs, packed a cooler, and wandered down to enjoy some live music as the sun dipped behind the Texas trees.

Between sets, we noticed a couple sitting about twenty yards away with the most energetic and cute little puppy. My wife was the first to approach (she's always very drawn to animals), and I wandered over about ten minutes later when I realized she was deep in conversation.

While she was talking with her new friend Nancy, I struck up conversation with her husband Richard. They were longtime Texans, so we had a lot to talk about differences in geography, people and life in general. We eventually asked them to move their chairs over to ours so we could enjoy the music and keep our conversation going. It ended up being a wonderful evening.

We didn't know them at all. But by the end of the night, we knew we had made our first real friends in our new home.

Since then, we've seen several concerts together, swapped stories over backyard drinks, and spent more than a few evenings just hanging out. All because we stayed open, curious, and said hello over a puppy.

Connection isn't about having extra time; it's about seeing and using your time differently. It's in the aisles, the waiting rooms, the hallway walks, and the festival field you didn't plan to visit. All it takes is noticing the opening, and being willing to lean in.

Chapter 10: Managing Your Energy and Expectations

Choosing Your Energy Level

You've seen how many chances to connect exist if you're open to them—at the gym (of course), in line at the store, even on a walk to the car. But even with all those opportunities, sometimes we simply don't have the energy. We're tired, distracted, and not in the right headspace.

That's why we need to talk about energy: managing it, maintaining it, and keeping our expectations real.

You don't have to be at full power to reach out. You just have to decide if it matters to you today. Try putting the action before the feeling. Whether it's a text, a short call, or a weekly game night—make the effort, even when it's small.

And it doesn't need to be local. You can find connection online too (young folks are nodding). Whatever the medium, you might discover that connection itself is what recharges you.

What you choose to do depends on your current energy, but it can also reflect where you want your energy to be. In the end, you should do what makes you feel the best about your interaction. Big isn't always better. What matters is that you choose something you'll actually do, and keep doing it. (Yes, just like your favorite workout. Had to sneak in one more.)

It also doesn't have to be only about you. You may find that other folks feel the same way and now you have a group of people actively looking to create connective activities. Then you tend to rotate ideas, locations, etc. and the planning is shared.

The type of interactions you do or even plan, are going to be dependent on how you're evaluating and managing your energy levels. Here are some easy examples of things that you can do from home ranging from low energy to high:

> **Toolkit: Active and Passive Connecting**

Getting off the couch

- **Quick drink (Low)** – Coffee, tea, or a bar drink with a friend. It's a chance to talk about the day, vent, or just catch up. These generally last only as long as the drink, so the time is completely up to you.
- **Get together plans (Low-Med)** – This can be inviting folks to come see you (which by the way is an excellent excuse to tidy up the house…), host a game night with snacks, or going out to dinner or an event.
- **Regular plans (Med)** – Think "date nights", movie outings, or trying out restaurants. I know people who make it a goal to never repeat a restaurant when they go out, which takes planning—but that's also where the fun is.
- **Creating regular events (High)** – This type of activity can be the in-person poker game, a local D&D game, coffee clubs, or anything in between. These take more coordination and energy to attend, especially with more people involved, but the payoff is bigger too.

Connections from the couch:

- **Quick Text (Low)** – Could be a short "Checking in on you", or "Was thinking of you, I hope you're doing alright".
- **Quick Call (Low)** – Much like the text. If you get voicemail, you leave a short message. If you reach your person, you may only want to call to set a time to grab some coffee or a beer.
- **Online call (Medium)** – You probably need to coordinate via text or calls to do this, but you can get a regular check in call with a family member or friend you've not seen. My wife

uses this very effectively with some of her friends in California as they'll set up virtual Happy Hours.
- **Scheduled Online Activity (Medium-High)** – This one takes more work since you're probably using text, email and/or calls just to gauge interest and get scheduling down. I did this a lot during the pandemic to set up online poker as a chance for people to connect, laugh and have fun.

Pandemic Poker

During the pandemic, I was determined not to hunker down alone with the family, so I arranged many online poker games. We jury-rigged an ipad so that we could see the other people playing and interact on a level better than just typing into the applications chat box. Yes, this took some work to do, but it helped all of us to not feel so isolated and it was very fun. I still have people wanting me to restart this up today!

This poker game showed that connection doesn't have to require a big outing or major effort. Sometimes the simplest, most playful moments are the ones that keep your tank full — especially when you're feeling isolated.

This doesn't mean you have to fill your full day even more full with outings. Not all interactions have to be live. I personally have several interactions where I am nowhere near the people I'm connecting with.

Which brings me to another favorite example:

Rolling Dice at a Distance

One of my favorite ways to stay connected is my weekly Dungeons & Dragons (D&D) game. I've been playing with this group since I lived in California, and when we moved to Texas, that threw a curveball at the game. We all still wanted to keep the bond strong and continue playing, so we adapted to the new reality.

We were already using our computers to manage the game maps, character movement and rolling, so all we really needed was a clear way to communicate and reasonable timing. My game master picked up a very good mic for the table in California, and we invested in good headphones for us in Texas. The schedule needed to alter a bit to allow for the two-hour time difference, but the sacrifices were worth it.

What matters isn't the tech setup—it's that on most Mondays I get to laugh and adventure with friends who live hundreds of miles away. The only energy cost is staying up a little later because of the time difference—and for connection, that's not a high price to pay. It's not about proximity. It's about showing up and managing your energy, even across a screen.

The Energy Barrier

That brings us to the *hardest* part of this whole topic—not just managing energy, but breaking through when you don't feel like you have any at all.

The modern lifestyle is filled with long workdays, endless errands, and family responsibilities. It really isn't a wonder that at the end of the day people want to stay in and recharge. The problem here is that if we wait until we're feeling up to it and fully energized to do something, we never do.

It's something I heard about writers: if you wait until you're inspired, you'll never really write anything. The trick is to write UNTIL you're inspired. That's the same trick we're talking about here.

When I was younger, I remember tagging along to my parents' bowling league nights. I was mostly there for the arcade games, but I never forgot the sounds of laughter and conversation coming from the adults. They'd also host poker nights or play card games I didn't understand. I'd sneak down the hall to listen—and wonder what could possibly be so funny about grown-up stuff. I get it now. That laughter was connection in motion.

Back then, doing things *with* people was just what you did. Not every weekend, but often enough to build real community. Compare that to today:

My generation came of age right when home entertainment exploded. I bring you (drum roll) the VCR. I still remember when my dad brought home the "magic box" that let us watch movies *on our own TV*. It was the most amazing thing I'd ever seen. Until game systems like Atari hit the scene. (*You can control the things on the screen? Mind-boggling.*)

Now we have endless options at our fingertips: streaming, online games, social feeds, you name it. And while that's amazing... it also means that staying in has become the default. We have so much entertainment **inside our homes**, that we sometimes forget about the joy of connecting with people outside.

Don't get me wrong, sometimes vegging out in front of a show is *exactly* what you need. But what if that's all you're doing? Weeks without some kind of social spark? That's when you start to feel the ache of disconnection..

So let me ask you: when's the last time you went out just to spend time with people?

Not for work. Not out of obligation. But simply because it filled your cup.

Chapter 11: When Connection Is One-Sided

You've got a good cadence now. You've been reaching out and managing your energy levels, and you're running on all cylinders. But what happens when, after all that effort…doing everything "right" … it still doesn't land the way you hoped?

That's part of the reality. Sometimes, no matter what you do, and through no fault of your own, the connection feels one-sided. Especially now, when ghosting or cutting people off is seen as normal instead of inconsiderate.

I believe in being the person who stays accountable, not because you always get a response, but because it defines who you are. Break the rules of "normal behavior" and keep showing up. It may be more work on your end, but connection isn't about collecting points for replies. It's about choosing to be the kind of person who builds and maintains relationships. That's the person others remember, trust, and often admire, at home, with friends, and especially at work.

Here are two moments where reaching out, whether or not it was returned, made a real difference:

Remote, But Not

I've talked a lot about things from my perspective, but I want to bring up how someone else's reaching out has impacted me. It starts back when I was working at a media company. I knew and interacted quite a bit with the technology folks since that was a large area of my responsibilities. Nonetheless, I got to know most of them pretty well on a personal as well as business basis. One gentleman, Dmitry, I said hi to and was friendly with, but we never really had a deep connection —at least at first.

Then, the pandemic hit. Within days we went from coming into the office daily to grabbing what we needed so that we could work remotely. Much like all of you, it struck me as an odd and unsettling experience. However, even without being able to "walk around" the office, I started doing a virtual walk-around and checking on people via our instant messaging tool. It wasn't the same, obviously, but for me it really helped me keep connection with people, which—given that we were all huddling in our homes—was incredibly important.

He was one of the folks that I reached out to. He was also one of the people who always responded. Over the months, we got to know each other better. We knew about our families and children. Their activities and challenges, etc. Strangely enough, I was a better friend with him than I ever was when I was just a short walk away in the office.

After the pandemic, I ended up moving out of state and working remotely from Texas. We kept up the practice of checking in with each other.

Then I got laid off.

That change basically eliminated our ability to speak via instant messaging. And here's where things happened that I did not expect at all. I had a lot of folks I talked to regularly and considered stronger friends, but after my layoff, they stopped interacting and responding. I'm not going to lie—that hurt.

Most of the people I thought I could count on disappeared into silence. But one person surprised me — Dmitry. Out of the blue, he reached out to me via text. He checked on my progress in finding a job, asked how I was feeling, and gave me encouragement. He wasn't responding to a message I sent. He did it on his own. The impact on me was incredible.

Honestly, even during my lowest points searching for work, those communications "strengthened my belief in humanity," so to speak.

I used to tell my wife I could live off one of his texts for a solid couple of weeks with a restored attitude and renewed hope.

It's been a couple of years since my layoff and Dmitry continues to surprise and delight me with his occasional texts and concern. His connections impact me positively every single time.

This wasn't about him reaching out during a hard time for me—how could he even know? His unbidden texts reminded me that connection isn't just about the reaching out. Sometimes it comes back to you, probably when you least expect it. And those moments stick with you.

It would be nice if that was the experience all the time. But it isn't.

What if the connection doesn't come back?

What if the silence stretches longer?

That brings me to another story.

A Friend in the Silence

This story involves a friend of mine, Lisa. I met her way back when we worked at the same banking institution. I won't bore you with the full history of our friendship, but she—like many others—I lost regular contact with after my family's move.

Lisa is probably one of the strongest people that I know. She's endured quite a bit by way of physical trauma, work challenges and emotional drama. Her endurance and her strength have always been something I've admired. She's been a good friend with solid advice and a keen sense of perspective.

As such, she's someone I reach out to more regularly than most. Most of the time, she's pretty quick to respond. Sometimes it's later. And then there was a long stretch where she didn't respond at all.

That's where I had to pause and check myself: maybe she only needed time, maybe something was going on. So instead of overthinking, I kept it simple—I'd offer a kind word, some support, and move on with my day.

I could have assumed she was ghosting me, like many people might today. I didn't. I kept reaching out, leaving a word of support here and there, and continued with my life.

Months later, she responded and we finally connected. The subject of that conversation isn't important. What mattered was when she told me that—even though she hadn't been in the right headspace to respond—my reaching out had been a constant source of support for her. That was a nice thing to hear. Sometimes the message matters even when the reply doesn't.

Now you don't always get that kind of resolution and proof to the impact of your reaching out. If you do, that's great, but chances are, the greatest bulk of your communications will result in no response at all.

That's why it's so important not to make it about the results, but about the action and your genuine feelings behind them—because every effort leaves ripples, sometimes reaching people at just the right moment, even if you never hear about it.

Toolkit: Keeping Respect

The best thing you can do is to remember to respect the other person's time and where they're at right now.

- **Detach from results** - A lack of reply doesn't erase the value of your effort. The joy is in the giving, not the receiving.
- **Keep it simple** - A kind word or quick check-in is enough. I find the longer the message you leave, the more you expect a reply. Short and genuine makes it easier for both of you.

- **Honor the silence** - Sometimes people aren't ready, or they're simply not communicative in the same way you are. That doesn't mean you stop caring — it just means your care shows up without strings attached.

Chapter 12: Follow Up or Fade Away

Connection, as we've seen, doesn't always give you feedback. In fact, most of the time, you're not going to get much at all. But if you never try again, I guarantee you won't get any feedback! That's why consistency matters so much—especially when it comes to following up. It's one thing to reach out once. It's another to keep showing up over time, even when you're not sure who's listening. That's where real connection lives. And that's exactly where we're headed next.

This is going to change depending on who you're talking to, but many times I literally send out messages to this effect "Hey there, I'm just dropping a line to say hello. I hope you're doing well!" Sometimes I get responses and this fires off a whole discussion and actual catchup with what's going on in each of our lives. Many times, as I've mentioned, people don't respond, but I always go with the belief that the check in is a positive item that occurs in their lives. It doesn't really matter that much of what you do say as long as you mean it.

Follow up is incredibly important because without it, your connections are basically the same as saying hi to a stranger you walked past on the street. There's no prize for having the most connections that don't know you. I'd rather have a small and solid group of people that I care about than hundreds of people who barely know me.

Now I can acknowledge that follow up can many times feel a lot like pestering. What if they don't want you to reach out? What if it is perceived as annoying?

These are natural thoughts that can come up especially if you don't get a response at all. This gets back to how your self-esteem and thoughts are as well as the reason you're reaching out. If you are in fact questing for a response, then I wouldn't be surprised if the person you're trying to connect with takes that as pestering, because let's face it… IT IS!

If you are reaching out with a genuine sense of caring for the person's well-being and want to send some love and support, I think it would take quite a bit of misunderstanding to think that you're pestering. For me personally, feel free to send all the love and encouragement texts and calls that you want! The more the better! So, much like the last chapter, you don't know what's really going on in people's lives. I figure though that it is better to be consistent than to end up forgotten.

One of my favorite examples of this comes from my own experience.

Coffee Anyone?

Prior to the pandemic, I used to get into the office very early to beat traffic. As a result, the only people in the office were generally the help desk team, the NOC (network operations center) team, and some folks on the creative team.

We'd gather and talk before the office filled up, on various subjects ranging from work issues and company strategy, to personal stuff going on in our lives. Then the pandemic hit.

It wasn't possible to gather like we used to. To combat that, I set up a weekly "Coffee meeting" where we'd gather online and talk. This meeting soon became the best meeting of the week for all of us. It was a place where we could interact with people not in our houses, share ideas or vent frustrations.

Fast forward to today. Of the original members of this coffee club, not everyone works at the same company anymore. That could have been the end of this and frankly I don't think anyone would have been surprised if it just faded out of existence.

It did not.

To this day we meet once a week. Sometimes everyone shows, sometimes there are only two of us, but everyone who attends STILL considers it to be the best meeting of the week. Our commitment to keep showing up for each other and keep this going has only deepened all of our relationships.

This experience validated what I've always believed: consistent follow up is a true sign of care. It builds a cadence of connection that adds to the relationships involved far beyond the circumstance and event itself.

Out of Sight, Out of Mind

Not every story has the same ending as my Coffee Club. For example, one of the people I grew close to within the operations team at the entertainment company I worked for just stopped talking to me after I left California. I've asked mutual friends if there was any reason—if I had upset him somehow—and they've all said no. But no matter how many times I try to reach out, I never get a response. And this was someone I thought of as a good friend.

As much as that stings, it reinforces the lesson: follow-up isn't about getting the result you want. It's about showing up anyway. Sometimes connections fade, and you don't get the why. But if you stop following up altogether, you guarantee the connection disappears.

Both stories point to the same truth: consistency matters. Whether it deepens bonds or leaves you wondering, the effort itself is the real act of care.

Keeping connections strong, especially across distance and today's breakneck pace, takes intentional effort. The enemy of which is procrastination. We all do it to some degree. At some point though, the bill becomes due and you have to deal with things.

So how can you get better at follow up? Good news is that most of the tools that you use to make connections are viable here.

> **Toolkit: Following Up**

- **Mark it on your calendar** – Physical or electronic work equally well, but don't underestimate paper. A wall or desk calendar stares back at you daily, a constant reminder—it's harder to ignore than a digital alert you only see when you open the app.
- **Using reminders** – Electronic tools can prompt you constantly, even down to the minute. Annoying? Probably. Effective? Definitely. It helps build the habit—but only if you let it.
- **Set regular times with someone** - When you really want to stay connected, especially with people you care about that aren't nearby. Pick a time and date together and stick with it. The frequency is up to you both, but the rhythm matters more than the length of the call.

My wife is really good at staying connected across distance. Since we moved to Texas, she has been away from her two chosen sisters. Working with their calendars and timing, my wife and her friends regularly get together for happy hours, sewing/project times (these are my favorite as they call these "stitch and bitch" … cracks me up every time), or special occasions.

In the end, the choice inevitably comes down to you. There are reasons when you and someone else are simply heading in separate directions. That's ok. It happens all the time. But if you really want to stay connected, then follow up is essential. Relationships most of the time don't end with arguments, they just drift apart slowly. Follow-up is continually paddling back to shore, rather than letting the boat drift downstream and disappear.

And even when you make the effort to follow up, sometimes you won't hear anything back. That's why I believe responding still matters more than we think.

Chapter 13: Why Responding Still Matters

In today's world, it seems like we ignore more than we take in. With the flood of information from news, phones, and social media, tuning out can feel like a natural defense against being overloaded—or more accurately, overwhelmed. Unfortunately, responding to messages and emails has fallen out of favor, with ghosting as the new normal.

Even though many people these days seem to dismiss it, the simple act of responding is underrated and highly important. Whether it's a friend checking in, a colleague asking for help, or a former coworker reaching out... it matters when you respond.

Now in no way am I saying that you need to respond to everything that happens in your life, or am I trying to hit you with a guilt trip to do so. Look, I know what it feels like to be ignored and have certainly done it to others (not proud of it, but there it is). What I am saying is that the very act of responding says more to the person on the other end than you might realize. You're not just sending a message back; you're building a level of trust and accountability with that person. Not only that, but you're showing that you are courteous, dependable and present.

Responding, by the way, doesn't mean you have to reply with all the information being asked. I'm sure that all of us have had a lot of things going on all at once and receive a text or call from someone right in the middle of the chaos. It is perfectly ok, to tell someone, "I need to call you back", or "I'll text you later, I'm in the middle of something." I know that this takes time, but it doesn't leave the other person hanging, and they know that you actually got their message.

As much as I've talked about responding, I know there are times when I've missed an email or text. Even when I'm feeling low energy, I try to take the time to go back and clear out emails and texts. Sometimes I find that I've not responded to someone for days. The first thing I do is to make sure that I do respond to their text or note and apologize for my delay. It always feels good to that person to have been at least heard and acknowledged. I know that there sometimes are situations where you're thinking… I don't really feel like talking to this person right now… I don't want to get into a long discussion. I think that's normal, and we all have feelings like that. But even the act of responding and telling someone that you'll connect another time; is a powerful way to let someone know that you still care about them and their time.

I personally try to stay in touch with a lot of people. Now, do they all respond back to me quickly, or at all? No. In fact, only 20% of them (think of the 80/20 rule) are actually good at it. However, even though I hold no judgments against those who don't respond, I whole-heartedly appreciate the ones that do.

My friend Will is a great example of this.

Always Accountable

I've known him for years since we worked at the same financial institution. We were colleagues of different areas within the same technology organization. He lived on the east coast, and at the time, I lived on the west coast. Still, we developed a good working friendship that later blossomed into a true one.

He was one of those people that I called as I "used my drive" when I had a 40-mile commute to work through LA traffic. It worked well because of the 3-hour time difference. I would be driving to get to work by 7am, which meant that I was catching him in the middle of the morning. Here's the thing though… I used to call to see if I could catch him, but most of the time, I got his voicemail, so I'd try and give him something to smile about and let it be. Will though, even if he couldn't talk that moment, or even that day... ALWAYS RESPONDED.

They ranged from "In a meeting, I'll call you later", to "this week is crazy, maybe talk next week?". Most of these were texts, but I also got some voicemails as well. To this day, Will is literally one of the most responsive people I know and we've only met live probably less than half a dozen times. His accountability gives me back my faith in humankind! (ok, perhaps a bit over the top...)

Responses don't need to be life-changing. Sometimes they actually can be, (you'll see in other chapters... wink wink...) but most often it is just the act of a simple acknowledgement.

It may seem small, but a simple reply can remind someone they're not alone. And that's what makes real connection.

Toolkit: Respectful Responding

A quick text or short reply is often all it takes to stay accountable. It lets people know you care enough to keep the connection alive. Here are some ready-to-use lines:

- "In a meeting — I'll call you back."
- "Can't talk now, but I'll check in later this week."
- "Saw this, thinking of you. More soon."

Chapter 14: The Power of Small Gestures

Small gestures. How can they help? They're small ... right? What's funny is how often the small that we see if just a part of something big that we can't fathom. Think of it the opposite way.

Big gestures generally involve a lot of energy, planning, etc. to pull them off. I have a lot of energy, but there's no way I have enough to do big gestures all the time. I would burn out.

Small gestures are powerful, because as I've said before, they are more likely to be something that you'll actually do. They also can have a disproportionate impact on the folks you connect with. For example:

Have you ever had someone out of the blue give you a compliment? Call you for no reason? Invite you to something for a change? Doesn't it feel great? I can go for weeks at a time on the memories of these seemingly small gestures.

A Small Ask, A Big Break

Here's a story about a small gesture that was definitely a piece of a larger puzzle. It was 1991, and I had just graduated college. I was ready for the whole "go to school, get good grades, go to college, get a good job and everything takes care of itself" mantra to play out.

Except it didn't.

I applied everywhere I could, went to temp agencies, and basically did all "the things" in order to attempt to get my first "real" job. A few weeks went by and I had nothing.

One day, I decided to walk around the corner to see if my friend Josh was home. We'd been friends throughout high school and I knew his entire family very well. His father answered the door and told me that Josh wasn't there. He asked me how I'd been and how job hunting was going. That let me release my pent-up frustration to a willing listener. When I was done, I said one thing that would change everything.

"If you could please keep your eyes open for me, I'd appreciate it."

Then I returned home and gave no more thought to it.

The next day, I got a call from Josh's father and said he saw something on the internal job board and if I'd get him a resume so he could send it on. I supplied him with one that evening and thought, *Well, that was nice.*

Two days later, I was at home, doing nothing really, when a phone call came in asking if I could come in for an interview.

I changed into my suit faster than Superman in a phone booth (ok, for you younger folks, that will make no sense, but ask your parents...) and went to the interview.

At the company, I did the standard talk with HR, then the hiring supervisor and finally with the Director of Accounting. The job was for was an expense report processor in the Accounts Payable department. The Director of Accounting pointed out that this wasn't exactly the type of job that fit my degree. However, I discussed (and lightly argued) with him that it would be a good foot in the door and experience for me.

Two and a half hours after arriving, I returned home exhausted. I flumped on my mother's bed and told her "If I didn't get that, there are no jobs to be had".

The weekend came and I tried to keep myself occupied to not think about the interview. Monday rolled around and the call came. I got the job. I started the next day. June 11th, 1991.

My career got started, and it all happened because of a small interaction a friend's parent.

You don't know what that small exchange will do. It could be huge like in my story, or it could just give someone a smile in a long day. Those small gestures can add up to something. Chances are, you'll not even be able to imagine how or where they'll go.

You don't always see the ripple in the moment. But small gestures are often the first drop that makes the whole wave.

Not every gesture has to be profound, emotional, or to serve a purpose. Sometimes, connection starts with something offbeat and maybe even a little ridiculous.

Alien Anthro 101

Back in college, I took my first (and last) night class. It was on Thursdays and 2.5 hours long. The subject was Anthropology. We started the VERY long class talking about the long path of discovery found in fossils, remains, and so on. For some, I'm sure this was fascinating, but it really wasn't my cup of tea.

Probably 90 minutes into this talk, the teacher had to step out. I looked to my left and right at the nodding heads trying to stay awake.

Out of the blue, I turned in my seat to face the student behind me. I'd seen him before around the business school so I knew he was likely in a similar major.

I said to him "You know what I think? I think aliens came down from the sky, crash landed on an island they called Atlantis and started the basic myths of the gods of the entire Mediterranean region". He looked at me blankly for about three seconds and then burst out laughing.

Bob became one of my best friends in college as well as a roommate for my junior year. Though we've not spoken in years, I know firmly that if we did, we'd slide right back into our friendship formed by a silly comment in a night class at Umass.

I know that not everyone has the personality to do this, but if you do, sometimes the strange makes for an even more memorable connection. That one ridiculous comment sparked a friendship that lasted years. It reminded me that sometimes the smallest, strangest gestures carry the biggest weight. You never know which one will stick.

Not all gestures are one-liners or big asks. Sometimes, they're just about being the kind of person who sees others.

No One Is Invisible

I was working in entertainment at the company I had joined after my long-term career in banking. The office was a long drive—about 40 miles one way—so I usually left early to beat traffic and arrived before most people.

The building had valets for VIPs visiting the executives. Each morning, I'd park, say hi, and head inside. Over time that morphed into me learning their names. A year later, I knew all the valets by name, and even a bit about their lives—whether they had kids, what they were into, and so on. They were great folks and fun to talk with. But wait, there's more.

Another group I got to know well were the security guards. I'd run into them on my way to lunch or when heading to the gym in the other building. I'd take a few minutes to chat, ask how their day was going, encourage them to take vacation when they said they had time but weren't using it. Before long, I knew all the security people in both buildings.

One day, the fire alarm went off. It was a standard fire drill. Per standard, we poured out of the building and walked to our designated spots a block away. The valets were outside, the security folks were directing traffic, and the rest of us were waiting for the all clear.

As we headed back, I was walking with my Finance team but also cracking jokes with one of the valets and giving the security crew a playful hard time. By the time we reached the lobby, my manager turned to me and asked:

"What are you? The mayor? How do you know all these people?"

I just shrugged "It's what I do". I like forming rapport with the people I see every day. For me, it's easier—and far more fun—than walking past with the uncomfortable silence of no eye contact.

None of these relationships formed in a day. They grew out of small, daily gestures that added up over time, and that made my work life far more enjoyable.

And sometimes those acquaintances start with nothing more than:

Two Words.

I was still at the same company, rarely at my desk. That didn't mean I wasn't working — I just spent a lot of time on the floor with the technology folks, attending meetings and getting to know them (what's a mayor to do after all?).

On my regular trips to the technology floor, I'd pass the same group of database administrators including a gentleman named Ted who I vaguely knew from some shared meetings.

Each time I passed, I'd say, "Hi, Ted," and he'd respond, "Hi, Marc." Simple. Over time, I started adding "Bye, Ted" on my way back to the stairs. At some point — I'm not sure exactly when — it became a thing. The "Hi Ted / Bye Ted" exchange was our running bit, and it never failed to bring a smile or a laugh.

Eventually, that silly ritual opened the door for real conversations. Through Ted, I got to know the rest of his group, and they joined in the joke. What started as two words became a daily moment of connection that made all of us smile — and still does even today. Ted and I don't work together anymore, but we've stayed connected and still text, always starting with the same "Hi Ted/Hi Marc." It makes me laugh every time.

You see, connection isn't a tactic—it's a lifestyle choice. I had nothing to gain from forming those connections other than the pleasantry of their company and building better work relationships.

None of these stories were large efforts. It's about reaching out in a small but consistent way that inevitably becomes who you are.

Try it out. Like we've said before, it doesn't have to be daily, it has to be yours.

If you're wondering where to start, I've included a list of small gestures in the Toolkit section: Simple, thoughtful things that take very little time but are easy to do.

The right gesture can say what words sometimes can't. But when the moment *does* call for words, there's one tool that builds trust faster than almost anything else: a well-told story.

> **Toolkit: Small Gestures That Stick**

Whatever you choose, keep it natural and authentic to you.

- **Start with two words** – A simple "Hi [Name]" is friendly, courteous, and often the first step toward real connection.

- **Drop a quick compliment** – Be genuine: "Cool shoes," "Great presentation," "Smart point in that meeting." Small comments leave a lasting impression.
- **Be the inviter (even once)** – Flip the script by being the one to call or ask someone to join, even if it's only for coffee.
- **Name + notice** – Learn someone's name, then build on it with little details over time ("How's the soccer season?").
- **The oddball opener** – Sometimes humor or a quirky comment breaks the ice better than small talk. Just pick your moments.
- **A quick ping (My personal favorite)** – Out of the blue, text "Thinking of you–hope your day's going well." Short. Genuine. Done.

Chapter 15: Storytelling as a Connector's Secret Weapon

Earlier, I talked about how it is possible to change, and even come to enjoy something you once feared. My high school experience proved that. But that wasn't the end of the story. Sure, I wasn't afraid to go first anymore, but that didn't mean I was suddenly a great speaker.

That realization came a few years later, in my 20s. I had been in the workforce for a bit and, while I'd never been to Toastmasters, I was aware of the classic no-no's of public speaking. The big ones? "Um" and "like." Most people use them as verbal fillers while their brain catches up to their mouth. But once you **hear** someone constantly say "um," it's all you hear…and their message gets lost.

That's when I finally understood one of the keys to public speaking: people are best at talking about what they know.

In a work setting, this usually comes naturally. You know your role, you're confident in your skills, and the words tend to flow. Sure, you might lapse into jargon, but that's normal. The real challenge is getting comfortable speaking when you're outside your comfort zone.

Presentation is Everything, and Everything— is Presentation

When I made that connection, I started to shift how I approached everything. I decided to treat **all** interactions as practice presentations. And I mean **all**—talking to a friend on the phone, giving a quick update to my boss, chatting in the grocery store, even leaving a voicemail. (As I've said before, voicemail is a great place to practice as most systems let you erase and redo the message if you hate it.)

Once I started doing this, I was practicing constantly. Did I get better in a week? No. But over time, the "ums" faded. My speaking became more measured. I stopped getting ahead of my own thoughts. And the best part? No one else even knew I was practicing. There was no judgment, simply quiet progress. These days, it seems people focus more on the loud opinions, while simple quiet progress is underrated.

Ok, almost no judgment. I had to learn how to judge myself constructively instead of beating myself up. I'd sigh in frustration when I left a rambling message or tripped over my words, but that's part of it. And honestly, I still have moments where I ramble or get tongue-tied. No one's perfect, so those moments don't bother me anymore. Remember: stick to what you know so you feel confident. Script things out if you have to. Use whatever tools help you stay grounded…

Comfort sounds like confidence, and confidence connects.

Of course, confidence is one thing. But what people remember? The stories.

Why stories? Because stories stick, in your memory and in theirs. If you think back on times in your life, I'll bet that a lot of them are memorable because of their story qualities. Have you ever had one of those times where everything goes wrong in the moment, but you think "You know, this is going to make a funny story someday"? It is so much easier to remember the key moments in your life if they can be retold as a story. Storytelling is less about sharing facts and more about sharing thoughts, feelings and experiences. Good experiences or bad, a story can help inspire or even make you more relatable as you show your vulnerable side.

When you show someone who you are on the inside, that's going to build a stronger connection than spitting out facts like text book. It shows people your humanity.

Here's an example that isn't really my story, but one where I was able to play a part in one that would help solve a serious work issue.

You can do that?

In one of my previous roles, one of our technology platforms was getting plagued with outages. Customer complaints were rising, and revenue was dropping. Not your optimal directions for business. The technology team was under pressure, but no solution seemed to be forthcoming. As the Finance partner for Technology, I could have just stayed out of it and focused on reforecasting while someone else figured out the problem. That's not who I am, and not how I do finance. I felt ownership with the issue... I had to do something. So, I started asking questions.

At first, it was informal chats. But eventually, I pulled the team together and asked a simple question:

"What would it take to fix this?"

They were hesitant. Possibly even shocked. They asked "You actually want us to talk about spending money"? In their experience, Finance people didn't ask open-ended questions like that. In their world, if it wasn't already in the budget, it wasn't happening, so they stopped asking. And in that moment, I realized this wasn't a Finance problem or a Tech problem — it was a connection problem. They needed someone to listen first, not say no.

But I wasn't there to say no. I told them to throw out ideas, even the crazy ones. No filtering. Just speak freely. I listened, most importantly, I connected with them as an ally to their cause.

One by one, they did. We notated, challenged assumptions, and came to a conclusion: what they really needed were a few high-powered contractors for three to five months. These folks could either directly solve the issue or stabilize the platform long enough for internal developers to fix it. From there, I helped shape the proposal and told the broader story of how the expense of these contractors was far less costly than the revenue we were already losing. Their openness with me made the risks and opportunities clear at the operational level, which in turn made it easier to translate the impact to the executives. Once leadership understood, they approved it—and the fix worked. The platform was hardened. Outages became rare. Everyone was relieved.

Looking back, that wasn't a standard budget meeting. It was a moment where I helped the team **find their story, and (more importantly) get it heard.** Given their history of dealing with Finance folks who always said no, building a connection of trust was huge. I didn't just let them go on their way either, I partnered with them so this was a shared presentation… and a shared victory.

Connection turned a budget meeting into a breakthrough. And that breakthrough didn't happen because I had the answer — it happened because I gave them space to tell their story.

And that wasn't a one-time thing. Again and again, I've found that the real magic happens when I stop talking and just stay curious. Here's one of my favorite examples.

Crazy Carnegie Mellon Kids

In one of my previous roles in Finance, I had to work with the legal department quite a bit, they handled the reviewing all our contracts. Part of the normal process for contract renewal as that it went through Finance and Legal before being paid. Being who I am, if I was curious about a contract, I'd walk over to the legal department and have a quick chat with the lawyer. One of the lawyers, whose name was Bryan, I worked with more than the others as he handled the technology contracts. I used to talk with him quite a bit when he had a cubicle, but when he moved to a shared office is when things changed.

Bryan had a bunch of pictures hung up on his office wall. This made sense. Of course he wanted his space to feel more like a home. It was a couple of these pictures that piqued my interest until one day I just had to ask.

"Bryan, what the heck is that contraption in the picture?" I asked. "Oh, that's buggy" he replied matter-of-factly. After giving him the sarcastic face of "Thanks, that explains everything", he proceeded to tell me what buggy was. I took a seat.

A little background is that Bryan graduated from Carnegie Mellon University (CMU). It was at this school where this *activity* was created. I'll let you Google the details later, but essentially it all started back in 1920 as a student race where teams create custom built aerodynamic pushcarts referred to as "buggies". Over time this racing oddity became a huge part of the school culture.

I sat spellbound by Bryan's description of this historic tradition that I knew absolutely nothing about. For CMU students and alumni, this is a huge event each year in April. In fact, Bryan had been a commentator at the event a few times.

What was the best part about this story? Watching Bryan light up while talking about it. He was so proud of it, his school, and this unique tradition that it had made.

In that moment, Bryan and I weren't just work acquaintances anymore — we were on the road to becoming friends. And friends help each other out. As a result, our work interactions were not only much more enjoyable, but we increased the speed of which legal review was done on my contracts, and he got immediate responses from me when he needed something. Storytelling is a secret weapon, and sometimes, the most powerful thing you can do is invite someone else to tell theirs. The work is always easier when you have connection.

You'll notice in both of these examples; the connection didn't come because I told a great story — it came because I asked questions that encouraged others to share theirs. And that's the real secret weapon of storytelling: sometimes the most powerful story in the room isn't yours.

So how do you tell — or invite — a story that connects?

Toolkit: Storytelling 101

Stick to what you know! You speak most naturally and confidently when you're sharing your own experience. Don't try to impress, just be real.

> **Be relevant** – The right story at the wrong time is still the wrong story. At work, a short anecdote that ties to the task or goal is perfect. In social settings, read the room. Not every story will fit in every moment.

1.) **Be true** – The best stories are the ones that really happened. Whether they ended in triumph or disaster, honesty makes them relatable.
2.) **Circle back to a point or question** – A good story can make a point, ask a question, or invite someone else to share. Try closing with something like, "Has that ever happened to you?".
3.) **Humor** – Embarrassing moments, small failures, or human quirks make great stories, especially when you can laugh at yourself. Humor builds trust and makes your story more memorable.

So, now if you're thinking, "I've got stories, but they're mostly awkward or embarrassing", don't worry. That might be your *best* advantage.

Let's talk about how humor and vulnerability take your connection game to the next level… on the next page 😊

Chapter 16: Connecting Through Humor and Vulnerability

Stories help people relate to you. But if you really want them to *remember* you? That's where humor and vulnerability step in.

Why humor?

Because life is serious *way* too often. And sometimes, the fastest way to build connection is to make someone smile. We remember the people who made us laugh way more than the ones who gave us grief.

Ever since my late teens and college years, I've held onto one core belief:

If I could make someone laugh, they had to like me—at least a little.

Was it true? Maybe not. But it didn't matter. What mattered was that *I* believed it. That belief gave me courage, especially when it came to talking to girls or building relationships of any kind. (Yes—for me, it all started with being able to talk to girls...)

That's when I came up with a personal mantra:

"The most important person in the world to amuse is myself. Anyone else who laughs? That's gravy."

That mindset gave me enough confidence to try. And over time, that "gravy" became part of how I connect with people everywhere I go.

I do this all the time now—probably because I can't help it, even if I should. I'll be in line at the grocery store, glance at the food someone's putting on the belt, and say something like, "Can I come to your house for dinner?" Just silly stuff. But it brings smiles. And you never know... something that simple could actually make someone's day.

Here's an example.

Unexpected Validation

I was waiting outside a local coffee shop for a friend. We have a consistently inconsistent habit of meeting for coffee and chatting. This time, I arrived a good 15 minutes early and was hanging outside, letting my drink cool, and enjoying the cooler morning air.

An SUV pulled up and backed perfectly into a spot across the way. Quick, clean, confident. And I thought, *That was pretty good. I should say something.*

Did I know these people? Nope. I just felt like giving a compliment.

A couple got out of the car and started walking toward the shop. I smiled and said, "That, sir, was an excellent job of backing in."

A huge grin spread across his face, while his wife rolled her eyes and said, "Oh no, I'll never hear the end of this."

I replied, "Consider yourself validated," and they laughed as they walked past. His smile got even wider. We all wished each other a great day.

That... was fun. A small moment. A quick connection. But I'll bet I gave him new material for stories about his *expert-level parking skills.*

Did I expect it to be funny? Not at all, but I was hoping it would be.

Humor crosses barriers like nothing else and really serves to disarm people in a real and gentle way. Moments like that are all around you. It is up to you on when and if you want to take that plunge.

Humor helps us connect in the light moments. But there's another kind of connection that runs deeper—the kind that happens when we let our guard down.

Vulnerability is tough. Why? Because we feel... well, vulnerable.

It is hard to throw yourself out there and share something about yourself. Now one could say, that's not so hard to share, but I'm not talking about surface level things like what baseball team you like. I'm talking about sharing something that is maybe not your best trait, a deep insecurity that you keep from the world... a fear.

But vulnerability isn't just about small admissions or silly moments. Sometimes it's about letting others see the truth behind the mask we've worn for years. So let me share you the truth about mine.

I was raised at the time when the formula for success looked something like this. Go to school, get good grades. Go to college and graduate. Get a good job and everything takes care of itself.

Except that it doesn't. Fact is, there is no formula for success that works universally. We all need to find the path that best suits us. I didn't always believe this. That's a sentence that's taken probably 40 years in the making for me to actually even believe, much less say.

I've always been driven by competition. Something that was rather difficult when you had three younger brothers who did practically everything better than you. There was no achievement of any sort that wouldn't be outstripped by my younger talented siblings. And though I eventually grew out of competing with them, the urge to push myself endured.

Competition, when used constructively, can really help you push yourself to new heights and move you on in your work. The problem is when it is used by yourself... against yourself.

Two Decades in the Dark

I was newly married, living in California. My wife and I were both working until our son was born when we made the decision (and sacrifice) to have someone be at home to raise him. As I was the one making more money and further along in a career, my wife took on the harder job of staying home, while I kept the job of provider. I wanted to give my family that American Dream. Have a good job, buy a house, drive decent cars, etc. Only one problem. My income was getting far outstretched by a housing market gone crazy. As much as I tried, I couldn't make that work, and the seeds of "not enough" were planted. Years later, after we had our second child, almost everyone I know owned a house, and seemed better off than we were.

Then, the housing and financial crisis hit and lots of folks lost their homes, but many still had them and I began to feel less and less. I would become very uncomfortable about going to people's houses if they had money. I compared myself constantly and chided myself for not doing enough.

"*I am not enough*" was my unsaid mantra. Though I continued to work extremely hard and advance in my career, I never seemed to get to that place where I could "make it" and relax. This negative thinking impacted me so hard one year that my health suffered, and mentally I was starting to doubt myself even at work. Fortunately, I was able to get through that with the help of my awesome family, friends, trusted coworkers (and you know who you are… thank you again, by the way), and a therapist.

Fast forward. As I write this, I still don't own a house. I don't drive an awesome car. I don't have a Swiss bank account with millions in it. But here's the shift: I stopped fixating on what I didn't have, and started focusing on what I did have. My focus stopped chasing the Joneses and realizing the wealth I had in my marriage (which is literally the best ever in my humble opinion), and my relationships with my wonderful son and daughter. With help from great people around me, I began to realize that I WAS enough, and that I could achieve what I wanted in life.

Now that all sounds miraculous except for the fact that it has taken me easily a decade or two to get to this place. But I wouldn't have arrived at all, if it weren't for the people in my life that I could be vulnerable with. The ones that didn't judge. They encouraged and eventually, I understood that no one could change me but me.

Being vulnerable helped me to let go and strengthened my ties to these people who were there for me.
I'm still striving to improve, and with a much better attitude now, I am more aware and grateful for what I do have rather than focusing on what I don't.
That certainly didn't happen as a flash of insight, but over time, I realized how important it is to know how to handle the darker seasons of life..

Just don't live there

I'm going to give you some advice that I gave my children about feelings. It's ok to feel badly, maybe even depressed sometimes.

Just don't live there.

Try to reduce the duration of those feelings, hour by hour to day by day. If this story resonated with you, I'm glad. I only hope you can find your own place of peace, maybe a little faster than I did.

Now that we've explored how to live the habit, let's talk about connection in the place where most people spend the majority of their lives — the workplace.

Section III: Connection at Work

We spend more waking hours at work than just about anywhere else. And yet, for many people, work is the one place they don't feel seen, valued, or connected.

That's a missed opportunity.

Building relationships at work isn't about climbing the ladder or becoming the office favorite. It's about making your days more human. When you have good people around you—people you actually know and like—work becomes less stressful, more fulfilling, and even, dare I say — enjoyable.

Whether you're in the office, working remotely, or somewhere in between, this section is about how to make meaningful connection part of your day-to-day work life. We'll look at ways to build better relationships with coworkers, strengthen trust with your boss, collaborate across departments, and show up in a way that helps you—and others—thrive.

Let's get into it.

Chapter 17: Connection in the Workplace – Why It's More Than Just a Job

Let's face it—work is one of the most consistent parts of our lives. But who really thinks of it as a place to build relationships?

I mean... it's work, right? We're here to do a job, get things done, and collect a paycheck. That's how it is for most people.

But what if work could be more than that?

What if it was a place you actually liked showing up to—not only for the work (and if you enjoy your work, awesome)—but for the people, the energy, and the camaraderie?

So why doesn't it feel that way?

Honestly, most of us are simply trying to get through the day. Deadlines, meetings, shifting priorities (you know how it is). It's easy to put your head down and treat the people around you like background noise. Add in remote work, office politics, or just plain burnout, and it makes sense that real connection takes a back seat.

But it doesn't have to.

Building connection begins close to home—with your teammates, your boss, and the groups your department regularly interacts with. Now, I understand that with different jobs this can vary quite a bit, but for the most part, I find that almost every group engages with at least two others, if not more.

Start with Your Boss: Questions Build Connection

Even when you're first starting out, it's important to get to know the people around you. These are the people you'll be working with, engaging with, and learning from.

So how do you start?

Questions are the key. You can do just what's asked of you, and deliver your work. But if you stop there, you're missing a golden opportunity to build trust with your boss, learn more about their job, see how your work fits into the bigger picture—and honestly, become that go-to person everyone relies on.

They say questions are the beginning of wisdom—if so, they're definitely the beginning of connection.

After working for several years and having had many bosses, I started to see some patterns—and remembered something my father told me when I first entered the working world:

"Marc, look for ways to take things off of your boss's plate, and work to make them look good. A strong boss will recognize you as a standout employee. And when they move on, you become the obvious choice for advancement."

Solid guidance. I mean what boss couldn't use less work to sort through, a great team and awesome work product? (Here's to you Dad…)

Over time, I added my own layer to that advice. I realized you almost had to read your boss's mind—not in some mystical ESP kind of way, but by really trying to see where their requests were heading, what they cared about, what pressures they were under—and then making sure you not only delivered what was asked, but anticipated what came next.

And what's the best way to know your boss's style and needs?

You guessed it: questions.

Now, there will be times when your boss truly doesn't have the time to explain a task because of an urgent deadline. It happens. In those cases, do the best you can (which you should always do anyway) and deliver. But once the dust settles, go back and ask the questions.

What was the result of the meeting? Who was there? What happened? These are simple, powerful ways to learn more about how the business works and how your role fits in. More importantly, they show that you're engaged and curious—and that kind of curiosity stands out.

Bosses notice when you care—not only about completing a task, but about understanding why it matters. And this is just the start. Next up, we'll go deeper into what it really takes to build that relationship—and how to approach executives too.

Build Real Relationships with Your Teammates

Let's switch to the folks who are really close to home—your teammates.

The people in the trenches with you.
The group that has to rely on each other to make things happen.

If you've ever been part of a great team, you know the feeling. When you've got high-powered people working in tandem, nothing seems impossible. Even the most stressful situations start to feel manageable. Teams pull for each other. And the more you know the people around you, the more you understand their strengths—and how to help each other succeed.

Questions still matter here, but let's be honest—no one wants to be interrogated by their coworker.

The trick is simple questions that spark conversation and show you care. Here are a few you can use to find common ground.

> **Toolkit: Questions to Find Common Ground**

A little small talk can go a long way when it's grounded in genuine curiosity. If you're not sure how to start, here are a few simple jumping-off points to find some common ground:

- **Work experience** – Where did they come from? What roles have they had? What did they study?
- **Geography** – Are they from here? Did they move for the job?
- **Entertainment** – What kind of music do they like? Do they read? Binge-watch anything? (I can't help but fire off 80's movie and music quotes myself)
- **Sports** – Do they follow any teams? Play anything themselves?
- **Travel** – Been anywhere interesting lately?

Sure, they may seem obvious, but sometimes those are the hardest to remember. And remember—the goal isn't to check boxes. This isn't a quiz. You're opening doors to real conversation.

You'd be surprised how quickly these kinds of questions lead to deeper conversations. Just talking about things that aren't personal often gives you real insight into who someone is.

But what happens when your coworker is from a different generation? Right off the bat, common ground sits on completely different timelines—what you find familiar might be foreign to them, and vice versa.

I get it. It can feel awkward to bridge that gap. But I've found that the best approach is simple: open your mind, listen, and learn.

Generational Adjustments

I was working at an entertainment company where my boss and I were about the same age, but the rest of our department was at least a decade younger. Now, my boss and I both love quoting movies and pop culture—especially Gen X staples. But after a while, we realized most of our references were landing with a thud. Not only were we missing the humor, but we were losing a key way we normally made points and connected with people.

So we adjusted. We started being more intentional with how we communicated. There was still humor—because that's our style—but we made sure it was something everyone could understand and enjoy. And it worked. The group started to feel more connected, and over time that generational gap began to fade into the background.

That time can vary. You may find your group spans multiple generations, with just as many different ways they prefer to connect. The first key is recognizing the hand you've been dealt. The next is finding the best way to communicate across those differences with clarity.

That may feel daunting, especially with a large team, but one of the best ways forward is surprisingly simple: ask questions. If you're not sure about a saying or a term… ask. Chances are, you'll learn something. And just like that, you've started a conversation instead of widening the gap.

After enough conversations, you'll have a much better sense of how to communicate with your team.

Find the Quiet Opportunities

Work can be a whirlwind most days, but there are quiet moments—if you're looking for them. A chat by the coffee machine, a shared lunch, even a hallway hello… these small pauses can open big doors. (And no, the bathroom is not one of them.)

And if you're remote? The "hallway" just looks different. A quick Slack message, a short Zoom follow-up, or a check-in email can serve the same purpose. The point isn't the location—it's noticing and using those moments to connect.

People often say remote work makes this harder. I don't entirely agree. It may take more effort than in person, but when you put in the time, the payoff is just as real. Remember *Coffee Anyone* from Chapter 12? That one is still paying off for me.

So whether you're in the office, hybrid, or remote, there will always be quiet moments. And honestly, we all need those breaks to function better. Keep your eyes and ears open—the opportunities are there if you're willing to see them.

Here's a story about a place I worked where opportunities were right in front of people, but most didn't notice them—let alone act on them.

Friday Gold

Back before remote work became the norm, I worked at a place that had very few employees in the office on Fridays. It was so common that my boss and I would make a friendly bet on how many people would actually show up during business hours.

So? That's not even a big deal these days, right?

What struck me wasn't the people who stayed home—it was the ones who came in. Of the few who did, a disproportionate number were senior leaders and department heads.

And that's the point: while most people worked from home, they missed one of the easiest chances to connect with accessible leaders. These situations don't come around every day. But if you were looking to build a stronger network, increase your visibility, or become the "go-to" person when no one else is around, then Friday offered a golden opportunity — one too many people left on the table.

I don't know what your version of *Friday Gold* looks like. Maybe it's taking an executive at their word when they say, "My door is always open." You may think they're just being polite, but I found out firsthand that some of them really mean it.

Stories like *Friday Gold* are just one example of spotting quiet openings. And if you'd like more practical ways to do it, I've pulled together a list of simple tactics in the Field Guide at the back of the book. Not every opportunity happens casually in the hallway—sometimes they show up in scheduled events where you least expect them.

Roundtable Roulette

Have you ever been invited to one of those executive roundtables—a "get to know you" session where a group of employees gets time with a senior leader? I've sat through several over the years, with mixed results. Some were genuinely interesting but left no room for questions. Others turned into little more than "suck up to the boss" time. Very few struck the right balance, and fewer still featured an executive who came across as genuinely real.

This story is about one that did. The executive—let's call him Roger—shared his background as Chief Accounting Officer (CAO) and then answered questions about the company. Since we were all in Finance, the conversation leaned heavily toward the business side.

What really struck me, though, was how Roger ended the meeting. We were on video from different offices, and he said, "If any of you have additional questions, feel free to reach out."

Now... I'll be honest. That sounded like a line—the kind of thing people say out of politeness more than intent. But I enjoyed the conversation, and I actually did have a few career questions I wanted to bounce off someone more experienced. So I took him at his word.

I reached out to set up a time. It took a couple of reschedules (he was, after all, the CAO), but we eventually connected for a one-on-one conversation. He shared advice, perspective, and ideas I wouldn't have had access to otherwise.

Even after I left the company, we stayed in touch. Roger is now someone I know pretty well—someone I respect, and who knows me, too. And all of that happened because I followed up on a simple offer.

Sometimes the door cracks open. If you're paying attention and looking for opportunity, you may get a chance to walk through it. And what you find on the other side? Well, that's up to you.

That's the thing about connection: it often shows up as an unexpected opportunity. Which raises the bigger question—why does connection at work even matter?

For me, it makes the day better. Work becomes more enjoyable when you actually like the people around you. It's easier to get through challenges, celebrate wins, and even laugh a little when the environment feels more human.

Shared experiences bring people together. They remind us we're not grinding away in isolation—we're part of something. The best jobs often feel that way not only because of the work itself, but because of the people we're doing it with.

And yes, connection helps your career too. We always hear that "networking matters," but it's not about collecting 500+ contacts on LinkedIn. It's about being known—really known. The kind of network that helps you grow isn't transactional. It's built on trust, shared effort, and people who've seen your work up close.

When managers or hiring teams are deciding who to promote or bring on, it's not only about skills. It's about fit. Will this person be a great teammate? Will they make the group better?

In my experience managing teams, that stuff matters. A hard-working team that gets along is more productive—and way happier. And happy teams? They crush it.

That's the power of connection at work.

Chapter 18: Connecting with Your Boss and Executives

During my time in the corporate world, I noticed that a lot of people tended to stay pretty removed from their manager. The only time they would interact—if at all—was during a staff meeting or when asked to perform a task.

And when it came to the executive team? Forget it. These people were far too important to talk to the likes of me (or at least that's how it seemed). But here's the truth: all of them are just people. And building relationships with them—when approached in the right way—can make all the difference.

Connecting with your boss isn't about sucking up or trying to curry favor. It's about building a relationship—one that can (and should) benefit both of you.

Your manager, at least in theory, has more experience in your field. That makes them someone you can learn from—someone who can help you grow, guide your development, and open doors.

I've been on both sides of this equation over the years, and one thing is clear: waiting for your boss to come to you is rarely the best strategy.

Most managers have a lot on their plate—multiple team members, projects, maybe even other managers they're responsible for. If they had to personally coach and guide everyone without any prompting, they'd never get their own work done.

That's why *you* reaching out first matters. It shows initiative, signals maturity and demonstrates ambition (the good kind). And maybe most importantly, it shows that you're willing to be taught. That kind of posture doesn't go unnoticed—and it can be a game-changer for your career.

The same goes for executives in your company. Taking the time to get to know them—not just as business leaders, but as people—is often a welcome gesture. These are folks who work incredibly hard and carry a lot of pressure. A thoughtful outreach or a curious question isn't only noticed, it's often appreciated.

Of course, executives are usually even busier than your boss, so respecting their time and being patient are essential. You might not always get a meeting right away, but making the effort puts you on their radar in a meaningful way.

This chapter is designed to help you feel more comfortable with that process—and offer a few paths to help you stand out as more than just an employee number. When it comes to connection at work, two groups stand out as especially important: your boss, and the admins who serve as the gatekeepers to executives. Each requires a different approach, so I've broken the tools into two parts.

The Exec Close to Home: Your Boss

It's funny—when you're first starting out in your career, you sort of think of your boss the same way kids think of their parents.
(Yes, I will explain this, and it will—hopefully—make sense.)

I didn't fully realize it until I became a parent myself. Kids don't see their parents as *real* people. They only see "Mom" and "Dad." Certainly not individuals who go out, have hobbies, or want to have fun. They're just… parents. (Parents? Having fun? Say it isn't so.)

I think bosses can get that same treatment. They're often seen as the ones who assign tasks, hold meetings, and hand out work—not as people who, like you, are doing their best to juggle responsibilities and take care of their families.

I'll admit it: I definitely didn't see my manager—or their manager—as real people for a long time. When I first started working, I was somewhat intimidated, if not downright scared, of my supervisor's manager. It was all I could do not to babble or get completely tongue-tied whenever I had to speak in front of him.

What I know now is that what made me so nervous wasn't that he was scary—he truly wasn't. It was the distinct confidence in his work, the kind that only comes from decades of experience and hard-earned expertise. And since I was brand new, the fact that he knew so much was intimidating.

Now, I'm not going to hit you with one of those "If I only knew then what I know now" speeches. The truth is, we learn through trials and over time. That's called experience. Incorporating that into your learning and becoming better as a result? That's called wisdom—and it comes with lumps.

Confidence tends to show up when we not only believe in what we're doing—but also in ourselves. There's no formula for when that switch will flip. (And anyone who says they *can* flip it for you is probably selling snake oil… or bridges.)

What I can do, though, is offer you some knowledge—something you can use to connect with and learn from others, and to put the experience of mentors and colleagues to work in support of your growth.

So why is it such a great idea to connect with your boss?
Can't I just do my work, leave the office, and go home to do the things I actually want to do? (Ah… Those were the days….)

Of course you can. That's entirely up to you.

But here's why I think it's a great idea: your boss is someone you literally see every day, and they're sitting on a treasure trove of experience and perspective—whether you like them or not.

I'm not saying you have to become best friends. But I will say this: when you're working for someone you genuinely like and respect, it's a total game changer. The work becomes more enjoyable—even during the crunch times—and the stress feels more manageable because there's trust.

And it's not just about learning how to do your job better. It's about observing how they do theirs.

My dad told me: "Always help your boss succeed." That sounds great—for them. But what about you?

Well, here's what tends to happen when you stay committed to helping your manager succeed: you start getting involved in more of how your department runs. You become the person your boss turns to when they need something done right. You become trusted. Known. Reliable.

And then, one day, you look up and realize... you're already doing their job. That's when promotion becomes easy.

Here's a little work-life secret: you don't get promoted *to* the next level. You get promoted when you're already doing the work of that next level.

It might not feel fair (and be honest, we know life isn't), but it makes sense. When your manager goes to bat for you, they're not taking a risk on someone unknown. They're putting their name behind someone who's already proven it. That's you.

So let's get to the how.

As we've talked about, connection takes time. That's still true when it comes to your boss. You don't need to become best buds on day one. Instead, here are a few things to keep in mind as you get started:

Toolkit: Keys to Working With Your Boss

- Patience – Building trust takes time. Don't rush it.
- Start with work – Your easiest entry point is the work itself. That's your shared context.
- Ask questions – The more you clarify up front, the easier your job becomes. Make it a habit to confirm what success looks like.
- Accept criticism – This one's tough. But your boss's role includes giving feedback—and not all of it will feel warm and fuzzy.
- Remember: it's work – This was a hard one for me. I used to take everything personally.

That last one deserves a story.

Perfection Paranoia

Early in my career, I remember how frustrated I'd get with myself for not delivering the "perfect" presentation. Every time I thought I nailed it, my manager would have changes. And even though I took it in stride on the outside, inside I felt like I was constantly falling short.

Over time, and after being a manager myself, I realized a few key things:

Style
I built the deck, but he was the one presenting. My style wasn't his, so of course he made edits to match how he communicated. (I know this sounds obvious, but over the years I've found that some of the most profound things are obvious, but only when you're ready to hear them.)

Black-and-white thinking
I assumed the goal was to deliver a polished, final product. But most presentations evolve. My role wasn't just to drop in

numbers and be done—it was to give him a starting point, something better than a blank canvas.

Options

By handing over the presentation in my voice, I was giving him something to work with, and options to choose from. What never occurred to me at the time was that he might not have known exactly what he wanted either. Giving him material to react to made his job easier.

Once I reframed it that way, I stopped chasing "perfect" and focused instead on being helpful. And that shift changed everything. Don't aim for perfect—aim for progress.

Another thing that helped me grow—both in confidence and career—was something that lined up with my habit of 'going first' (more on that in Chapter 20), but in a work setting.

Sooner or later, you're going to be asked to take on a project or task that feels above your head. Something that makes you hesitate. Your first instinct might be to say no, to explain that you don't have the experience, or even suggest someone else for the job.

I've been there. And what I've learned is that those moments—when your first reaction is "I can't"—are usually the exact moments where growth happens *if* you're willing to lean in.

Lost but Willing

By this time, I'd been in the working world for a good ten years. I'd even been promoted into management.

(Quick aside: if you think you'll have it made once you get to the next level... think again. Most of the managers reading this are probably nodding while wistfully remembering the days when they only had to think about their work before heading home.)

I sat in my manager's office while she laid out a new project she wanted me to take on. I won't get into the specifics—because it was a Finance project, and trust me, it would bore most of you to tears.

The point is this: as she explained the task, a slow-burning panic began building in my gut. I was nodding along, taking notes, doing my best to follow—but inside my brain was screaming:

I have no idea how to do this.

I could have spoken up. Could have admitted I wasn't sure how to get it done. But instead, I held my tongue. I was finally learning that my first reaction to things... wasn't always my best one.

So, with a stomach full of nerves and a low-grade feeling of nausea, I left her office.

I opened a blank Excel file and just stared at it. Then back at my notes. Then back at the screen.

How the hell am I going to do this?

That thought kept rolling through my brain like a broken record. But eventually, I made a decision: this wasn't going to be solved through mental gymnastics or ESP. I had to start doing something.

So I began building the spreadsheet.

As I moved, ideas started to come. One after another. When I hit a wall, I walked back to my boss's office and asked questions. Did she think I was failing? No. Absolutely not. She welcomed the questions, gave thoughtful answers, and made a few directional calls based on what I was building.

I went back to my desk not only with answers—but with renewed confidence.

Long story short: I finished the project. It took a couple more check-ins to clarify a few things, and sure, she still made changes to finalize it. But by that point I didn't take that personally anymore.

I felt on top of the world.

I had just solved something I never thought I could. That moment gave me something I carry with me to this day:

"I will always solve the problem."

It sounds simple (and probably a tad arrogant), but it changed everything.

From that point forward, the panic started to fade. The more "above-my-head" projects I got, the more I replaced fear with faith. I trusted that I'd figure it out—because so far, I always had.

And it taught me another valuable lesson:

Keep moving.

Sitting still and overthinking wasn't going to solve the problem. But action—even uncertain, imperfect action—got me unstuck. And once I was in motion, things began to click.

Working closely with my boss, asking questions, understanding their style, and letting go of the idea of "perfect" helped me build confidence that carried me through my career.

Lost but willing. It's okay to be nervous—even afraid. The goal is to try, and to learn that the combination of questions, trust, and imperfect action can change how you work forever.

The Closed-Door Boss

Now, all of this sounds great if you've got a manager who's engaging, supportive, and available to connect with.

But what if you don't?

What if your boss is distant, distracted, and not exactly a natural when it comes to managing people? What if they seem more focused on checking boxes than building up the people around them?

These are real situations—and they happen more often than we'd like to admit.

I'm not excusing those managers, but I will say this: you never really know what's going on behind the scenes. They might be overwhelmed, working on projects well above their comfort zone, or simply struggling to keep their own head above water. Or maybe they're just not the kind of manager you naturally click with.

So what do you do?

Here's something I've learned: even if your direct manager isn't someone you can easily connect with, that doesn't mean all is lost. You have options.

In fact, some of the most meaningful relationships I've built at work came from outside my reporting line.

You might be surprised to find that the executive a few levels up—the one you only see at town halls or catching a quiet moment in the break room—is actually approachable, funny, and generous with their time.

Executives are people, just like you. They may have more experience and carry bigger responsibilities, but that doesn't mean they're off-limits. If anything, many of them want to connect. They just don't often get approached in a genuine, respectful way.

So if your direct manager feels out of reach, look elsewhere. Make sure your manager knows about the interaction, so it's seen as supportive rather than as you going over their head. The last thing you want is to create embarrassment for your boss.

Executives in your company can be just as, if not more, valuable when it comes to learning, growing, and finding advocates for your work. That's why connecting with them deserves its own focus. Let's head there next.

Secret Door to Executives

Here's another bit of advice my father gave me early on in my career—and it's one I've never forgotten.

He told me: "Never, ever look down on or discount the administrative assistants."

(They were still called secretaries back when I started, but you get the idea.)

He went on:

"Marc, the administrative assistants (admins) are the gatekeepers to the executives. They control the calendars, the meetings, the trips—they organize those leaders' entire workdays so they can actually get things done. No matter how nice the executive is, if you get off on the wrong foot with their admin, you may find it impossible to get time with them. So be kind. Be friendly. And respect the important part they play in an organization."

And he was absolutely right.

Again, I'm not talking about buttering people up simply to get in the door. That kind of flattery will backfire fast. People—especially seasoned admins—can see through fake behavior in an instant.

Even early in my career, I kept that advice in mind. Much like the executives themselves, admins can be hard to get to know at first.

You may not interact with them much—especially early in your career. But like with any other relationship, it starts by being intentional. Here are a few ways to start:

> **Toolkit: Keys to Working With Admins**
>
> - **Create opportunities** – If your boss needs something sent to an executive, offer to hand-deliver it. Make an effort to say hello and learn their names.
> - **Stay curious** – Ask how long they've worked with their executive. What do they enjoy about it? What's one of the most interesting parts of the job?
> - **Show kindness** – If you see them buried in work, offer a coffee run. Even the smallest gesture can leave a lasting impression.
> - **Practice patience** – Executive calendars change on a dime. That open slot you were promised? It might disappear without warning. Don't take it personally—it's not about you.

Kindness Clears Paths

When I was working in entertainment, part of my Finance portfolio included the Technology division. I engaged in their staff meetings, managed forecasts, handled variance analysis—you get the picture.

To better understand the division and its leaders, I made sure to set up 1-on-1 meetings with key players. One of those was with the Chief Technology Officer (CTO). As you might imagine, rescheduling was a constant event. I'm talking "five-minutes-before-the-meeting" type of rescheduling.

So I got into the habit of stopping by the CTO's office about 10-15 minutes before our meeting—just to check in with his admin, Mary.

Mary was kind, funny, and sharp. Even if she told me the meeting was going to need to move, we'd usually have a few minutes to chat and connect. Over time, that regular check-in turned into a real rapport.

Then one day, I didn't only want to talk to the CTO—I **needed** to. We had a vendor situation in the tech division that required his authority to resolve. Every day we delayed was costing the company real money.

I checked his calendar—wall-to-wall meetings. No room at all.

I didn't email. I didn't call.

I walked down to Mary.

It was early in the day, and I explained the situation. Without skipping a beat, she looked up at me and said, "For you? I'll get you in. Don't worry."

And she did. The issue got the attention it needed, and just like that, it was resolved.

How did that happen?

Because I took the time to build a relationship with someone people often overlook.

She knew me. She knew I wasn't trying to work an angle. And when I genuinely needed help, she came through.

That's the power of the secret door: when every other option is closed, connection can open one.

Grace and Saving Face

While we're on the subject of kindness, it's important to know that you're going to have days that just get to you. You'll feel hot under the collar and want to put whoever's opposing you in their place with a solid, rational point.

If you'll recall, I said early on that *"the situation is not more important than the relationship"* is one of our family mottos. But it's hard to hold to that when someone is blatantly against you in a meeting.

So what do you do? Most of the time, I've seen it play out where one person does, in fact, set the other down. The argument and the point are won—but the relationship has been damaged from that point forward. That's how you end up with entire departments that don't work well together. They stop seeing themselves as essential pieces of the same company and instead view each other as opposing camps

Is it bad to win an argument at work? No, not at all. What's important is not to back the other person or the other team—into such a corner that they can't save face. That's what people hold onto long after the situation is over. Months or even years later, they may not remember the issue, but they'll remember how it felt to be embarrassed and not allowed to leave the moment with dignity.

This requires you to exercise something that's not often talked about in business: **grace**. It means finding a way to pull the other person out of that corner and give them a path back to neutral ground.

Here are a few ways to do that:

Toolkit: Keep the Relationship

- **Give them credit** - Find something in the conversation that credits your opposition. "You've brought up some good points that have given me things to consider."
- **Acknowledge the tension** – One of the best ways to diffuse a situation, is to state it out loud. "I know this has been a tense discussion. I appreciate your partnership and willingness to bring up alternate options."

- **Bury the hatchet** - Once things have cooled, make a point to go back to that person and work it out directly. This is especially important if you have to work with this person or group often.

This is difficult to do, but if you can manage to allow someone to keep their dignity, you'll likely find that they'll continue to work with you—and respect you even more for it.

These same principles hold true even when there isn't an argument to be won. Always work to make people look good if you can. Never embarrass them—especially not in public, and particularly not your executives..

Now let's look at how we connect with those executives at different stages of your career.

Connecting with higher levels at all stages

Stage 1: Early Career – Just Getting on the Radar

This is probably the hardest stage to make meaningful connections. Let's face it you're new, and you know almost no one. Your experience level is essentially just booting up and you're ready to take on inputs.

So how do you connect with higher-ups when you're just starting out?

First of all, don't expect to build a real relationship with a senior leader on day one (unless they go golfing with your dad or are friends with your mom, this is highly unlikely). It takes time. Your first meaningful connection usually won't be with an executive anyway. It'll be with your direct supervisor or manager.

Whether you're confident or quiet, I've found that your ability to connect early on usually comes down to two things: the work, and your approach to it.

My dad always told me, "Outwork the other folks." He didn't mean working unnecessary hours, though he did support putting in more time if the situation demanded it. What he really meant was finding ways to do the job better—make the process smoother, improve the output, and think ahead. And that last part matters most: thinking is what bosses and companies are really looking for. Anyone can do rote work. Thinkers are problem solvers.

I've never had a manager turn down an offer to make a task more efficient or accurate. Most people only do the job as it's handed to them. But when you take initiative to improve the work itself, you get noticed. And being noticed, in the right way, is the first step to being trusted.

Let me give you an example from one of my first jobs.

Stand Out by Showing Up

I was brand spanking new, 21 years old, and working in the accounting department. (Try to contain your excitement.)

The company was about to replace its entire financial system. And when I say entire, I mean all of it. General ledger, journal entries, accounts payable, treasury, everything was changing. Naturally, this kind of overhaul came with its share of problems, and the company needed people to help test the system before it went live.

They put out a call for volunteers to come in on weekends and run user tests. Our job was basically to try and break the system. Stuff like entering unbalanced journal entries (all my accountant friends just flinched), flipping the debit/credit signs, you name it. If it could go wrong, they wanted us to make it go wrong so the implementation team could fix it.

I had plenty of ideas about how I'd rather spend a weekend, but I also saw this as an opportunity. Not for a raise or a title, but a chance to show some initiative. And I did. I showed up, ran test cases, asked questions, and learned a lot in the process. Not many people volunteered, so my participation got noticed. It didn't launch my career overnight, but it was appreciated, and it gave me an inside look at the system I'd be using. More importantly, it was my first real step toward building trust, credibility, and connection. And it started me on the path of building consistency.

That's the key.

You might get noticed for doing something once. But if you make initiative a habit? You can't help it—you *will* be seen..

And once you're seen, that door to connection opens. So make sure you stick your foot in that opening and keep it there! That's how communication with leaders—and real connection—starts.

Stage 2: Mid-Career – Getting in the Room

By this time, you've been around the block. Solid knowledge, a healthy degree of confidence, and maybe a little swagger. (not too much—that tends to turn people off). You're no longer a rookie. You've become a proven commodity, and people see you as a valuable asset on the team.

If you've really been doing well, you're not only talking to your boss about how to accomplish the tasks coming out of an executive meeting… you're actually in the meeting.

Welcome to the room.

Now what?

Not that we're checking boxes here (bad habit), but once you've been noticed, this is the time to shine by showing your value beyond just the job description.

So how do you do that?

Good question. It reminds me of a quick hallway conversation I had with an executive about 10 years into my career. We were talking casually when he said:

Quest for the Big R

"In my career, I've found that everything comes down to responsibility... the Big R. If you want to move forward from wherever you are, look for opportunities to take on more responsibility. Increases in the Big R end up turning into promotions—and increases in the Big $."

That hit home. When I combined that with my father's maxims, the path forward became clearer: do great work, make things better, and take on more.

That's how you get noticed—and that's how real connection starts.

Remember earlier when I mentioned my dad's advice: "Always help your boss succeed"?

Here's the tactical part of that.

If you take my father's advice and combine it with what that executive told me about taking on more responsibility, then the answer becomes pretty clear:

Find ways to take work off your boss's plate.

Obviously, you'll need to have some bandwidth to do this. But again, I've never met a boss who wasn't thrilled to hand something off to a trusted team member—especially if it frees them up to focus on higher-priority decisions.

And here's the kicker: as your responsibilities grow, your boss will likely have you speak to the parts of presentations you worked directly on. This is a good thing. A natural growth step. It gives you visibility, credibility, and the opportunity to not only listen to executives... but interact with them.

(What do you mean interact? I just want to present and get out!) Trust me—I've been there.

But here's the deal: they will ask questions. Sometimes right in the middle of your presentation. Sometimes before you even finish your first slide. You might get through your whole section unscathed... but don't count on it.

And that's okay.

You just have to remember this: the point isn't to survive the presentation—it's to add insight. To help executives do what they're in the room to do: **make smart decisions quickly.**

If you can become someone who helps them do that? You'll be invited back.

And the more you're invited, the more comfortable you get with them—and they with you.

Hmm... sounds like connection to me.

Stage 3: Established & Trusted – Building Real Relationships

You're long past discomfort with the room. The consensus now is that you're a valued partner—not just in the room, but seated at the table.

Your words carry weight.

Your insights matter.

And you're no longer talking at executives—you're talking with them. (That's a huge difference.)

Some of the executives might even like you.
(It's okay if they all don't. At this stage, being liked is nice. But being respected? That's what really matters.)

Now is the time to expand your focus. Stop thinking only about your own area or function. Start thinking about how you—and your team—can help other parts of the business succeed. When you do that well, you're not just a trusted contributor anymore. You become a connector of people, ideas, and solutions across the company.

And that means more time with executives than just at monthly status meetings.

You'll need to be observant. Learn their styles. Pay attention to their rhythms, their communication preferences, their quirks. What frustrates them? What energizes them? What do they consistently care about?

I was well into my career. I knew my craft, had an abundance of relationships with my technology leaders, and was just at that point where I was starting to be *"at the table."*

Executives, just like people (which they are), come in all kinds. Most are drivers: ambitious, decisive, and high-energy, each with their own style of managing their area.

But I distinctly remember one who always stood out to me.

Confidence is Contagious

He just seemed genuinely friendly. I had never seen him without a smile on his face. He had a booming voice that carried, and I never heard him utter a negative comment.

I certainly didn't have that kind of confidence yet, so I made a point to get to know him.

Chuck was a heavyset man with an almost jolly disposition. (No, I had not found Santa.)

I made sure to work with his admin—as we discussed earlier, this is very important at all stages—to set up some time.

That first meeting turned into many more. Over time, those conversations evolved into a relationship where I was welcome to just pop in. Chuck was always generous with his time. He talked freely about how he got to the executive level, and he was a great listener. Sometimes he helped me vent. Sometimes he helped me see things in a different light.

And it wasn't only me.

His team was high-performing. They were dedicated, loyal, and energized under his leadership. They *loved* him.

Chuck was an executive who never lost who he was. He was confident, competent, and kind. If you didn't like that? So be it.

He didn't change for the title, and because of that, he earned both the title *and* the trust.

Chuck was the kind of executive I hoped to become.

This isn't just an executive thing, by the way.

You'd be amazed how far a small moment of human memory can go. Let's say you remember something they mentioned in passing a week ago:

"Hey, how's your sister doing? I remember you said she was recovering from surgery—has it been going okay?"

Little things like that work at *all* levels. They show that you're not talking to someone's *title*—you're talking to the *person* behind it.

That kind of connection? That's what builds the kind of trust that doesn't show up on an org chart—but makes all the difference.

Chuck might not have been Santa—but his gifts of time, knowledge, and solid advice made him just as legendary to me.

Connecting with your boss or executives might feel intimidating early on, but it's one of the best habits you can build. These relationships matter at every stage of your career. Just remember—they're people. Treating them with kindness and respect never hurt anyone, and it almost always helps.

Chapter 19: Top Down - Leading with Connection

How Great Bosses Build Trust, Loyalty, and Buy-In

Executives...
Thought you were going to get out of this?
Not a chance.

In fact, how *you* connect with your team, not just your direct reports, but everyone in your area, isn't only as important as what your employees do to connect upward.

It's *more* important.

Why do I say that?

Because in all my years of working across teams, functions, and org charts, I've seen a pattern repeat itself over and over.

The culture of a department almost always reflects the style of the leader at the top.

If that person's a micro-manager? You can feel the tension ripple down.
If they're a teacher who builds people up? You can feel the lift.

It's not just about work style, it's about personality, too. Just like we talked about with Chuck, a positive, grounded boss can make the work lighter for everyone. You walk into those teams and you *feel* the difference.

Now, I know all the *good* bosses out there already understand that buffering your team from chaos and stress is part of the job. But *how* you do it? That's what separates a manager from a leader.

In one of my previous jobs (which shall remain nameless), I worked under an executive who led with a micro-style, seat-of-the-pants energy.

Everything was a crisis.

That kind of leadership stresses people out and can wear down a team fast.

But here's the thing, I didn't report directly to him. I reported to the person right underneath him.

Boss, Leader, Friend

And that man's name was Bill.

He was charismatic, calm, and the complete opposite of a micro-manager. He knew he had smart, capable people working for him — and he treated them that way. We had autonomy. We had ownership. And most of all, we had his trust.

The only time he'd step in directly was when something needed to be rolled up for corporate. Otherwise, we owned our areas, made our decisions, and reported honestly on the outcomes. And because of that, we thrived.

Bill laughed easily and was instantly likeable—not that he needed to be. On our small team, titles didn't carry much weight. Everyone had a part to play, and he treated us like professionals, not rank-and-file resources.

He was also a fantastic teacher. I learned more from him about aspects of business operations and strategic thinking than I had in years prior. And he welcomed ideas and opinions from anyone on the team … regardless of role.

But what made him truly special was how he buffered chaos.

We were downstream from a crisis-prone executive, and yet? We didn't feel it.

Bill didn't freak out. He didn't pass stress down. He gathered his team, laid out the goal, and let us do what he knew we could do. He shielded us from the noise and cleared the path so we could execute.

And we did.

A good leader, even if they're not at the top of the org chart, can completely transform the team's environment.

Bill did that in spades.

To this day, I consider him one of, if not the best boss I've ever had the pleasure of working with. He didn't set the company's culture. But he sure as hell set ours.

That's what I want to stress here—leadership isn't reserved for the top. It shows up wherever someone decides to lead.

Leadership Impact – Communication

Communication is essential to any good relationship. That's just a given.
But the way a leader communicates? That's a whole different story.

One small comment from a senior executive can set off a ripple effect that spirals into a hundred hours of unnecessary work. What might have been a quick check-in with a direct report can suddenly turn into a thousand people scrambling to produce a report no one really needed. (I've seen this, and it's not pretty).

A friend of mine once told me a story that perfectly illustrates how miscommunication can spiral. I don't know if it's true, but the lesson holds.

The Ordinance Report

A general was at an army firing range, touring with his staff. Looking out over the troops, he casually said, "I wonder how much ammo we go through in a day?" Then he continued on his tour.

One of his lieutenants took the comment as a request—maybe even an order. He scrambled to pull together data, enlisting the base commander, quartermasters, and firing range staff. Because the general was visiting multiple bases, the lieutenant had those bases working too.

By the time the tour was over, the lieutenant handed the general a thick binder titled "Ordinance Report." The general flipped to the last page, glanced at the number, said "Oh..." and closed it. He had only been curious.

The point? The general needed to be clear about what was an idle thought versus an order—and the lieutenant needed to clarify before turning dozens of people's lives upside down for weeks.

Lots of wasted time and effort comes from that grey space between top leadership and middle management. It's like there's always a fog hanging there, making it hard to see.

A quick clarification—just a simple question—can clear that fog in seconds.

Leaders have to think about their communication **all the time**. As illustrated in the story above, clarity is crucial—not just when managing down, but when managing up and even collaborating across.

The method may change depending on the direction, but the need for clarity never does.

Prioritization through Visualization

When I was working in manufacturing, I had a boss who loved to swing by my office and drop off the latest project he wanted done. That was his prerogative, of course, but after a while, it started to create a confusing jumble of priorities.

He was always very clear about what he wanted and why.
But when? That was anyone's guess.

Without any big-picture guidance, I assumed whatever he gave me was the new top priority. Turns out, that assumption was... flawed.

He knew I had multiple projects, but without a visual cue or a shared tracking system, he left prioritization to me, which meant I was stuck guessing. And I was guessing wrong and starting to waste time.

So, I adapted.

My approach?

The Whiteboard Lesson

I grabbed my whiteboard and wrote out a list of active projects, their priority order, and estimated completion dates. It was originally meant to give me a little sanity and a sense of my bandwidth—but it turned out to be even more helpful for him.

Not long after I put the board up, my boss came in with a small new assignment. I told him I could absolutely take it on, then pointed to the whiteboard and asked,
"Where would you like this to go on the list?"

He looked at the board, rubbed his chin, and said,
"Never mind,"
and walked out.

He wasn't mad. I wasn't refusing work.
But the message got across.

That simple visual cue helped him realize what was already on my plate—and gave him the context to make a better decision. Not just for me, but for the whole team.

Communication styles vary.

In this case, my tool was nonverbal, but it worked.

The key is for both the employee and the leader to find what works, and communicate it clearly. Doing so eliminates confusion, saves time, and sets shared expectations on both sides.

Communication = Connection = Efficiency

Spidey Wisdom

As Spider-Man taught us: "With great power comes great responsibility."

That's the kind of power a leader has—sometimes without even realizing it. With a passing comment, emergencies can be created. With a clear guiding plan, a team can stay focused and avoid wasted effort.

Communication has long been called a leadership skill, but I think it's more than that.

It's a responsibility.

A requirement.

Your teams are looking to you, not just because you have the title, but because your words carry weight. And how you throw around that weight? That can be the difference between a high-functioning team and a mediocre one.

Leadership Style – They're watching you

Okay, that sounds a little creepy—but let's face it.
You *are* being watched.

The executives you present to? They're not just looking at your charts. They're watching how you carry yourself. (Ok, scary at first, but you get used to it)

Your cross-functional peers? They're noticing how your team communicates and supports each other. And your employees? They're watching *everything*. Because you're closer to the company's big picture than they are, and your behavior becomes the barometer for how things are going.

Want an example?

Stress Without Saying a Word

Ever been sitting near your boss's office and suddenly hear her coming from a mile away? Sharp footsteps. Tight expression. She walks straight into her office and closes the door with authority. No words. Just that.

That's business for "something's wrong"—and it's probably a doozy.
(That means a big one, for all the younger folks.)

So how do you think the team feels while she's in there, and when she comes back out?

Well, I can tell you one thing: It is *not* happy.

More like tense, stressed, anxious and perhaps with a dash of panic.

It could have been a great day up to that point.

Now everyone's sitting on pins and needles, waiting for the inevitable staff meeting that's definitely not going to be fun.

Of course I don't blame her for having emotions. But I doubt she realized the impact she was having on the team in that moment. And that's the point.

Leaders *need* to think about these things.

Everyone gets overwhelmed. Everyone needs ways to cool off. But when you're the one setting the tone for the team? Managing those moments becomes twice as important.

> **Toolkit: Managing Stress**

Here are a few quick resets that have helped me (and leaders I've worked with) keep from passing stress down to the team:

- **Find a quiet spot and breathe** - Yes, I know—you're on a deadline. But rushing in while frazzled won't make it better. A few deep breaths can reset everything.

- **Take a real break** - Grab five minutes for a snack, water, or coffee. Step away from the chaos, just for a moment.

- **Do a quick self-check** - See yourself. Literally. Step into the restroom and look in the mirror. Are you flushed? Tense? Distracted? If you wouldn't want to be on the receiving end of that look, take a little more time before going back into the fray.

If you take a few minutes to ground yourself, the walk back to the office doesn't feel so ominous.

And your closed door doesn't turn into a beacon of dread for your team.

You'll feel better.
And more importantly?

Your team won't start the day on the back foot.

Because stressed teams don't perform like happy ones.

Leaders set the culture

Let me be clear: I'm not writing any of this because it's easy.
I'm writing it because it's true.

Awareness is where real change begins. And leaders, more than anyone else, have the power to shape that change, for better or worse, on a scale that most people can't.

It may seem counterintuitive, but the "culture" of a team, a department, even an entire company, doesn't come from the thousands, or tens of thousands, of employees.

It comes from the top.

Leaders guide it.
They mold it.
Leaders shape what's acceptable, what's rewarded, and what's ignored.

People take their cues from the ones in charge. And over time, those cues turn into norms. Norms become habits. And habits? That becomes your culture.

We talked earlier about Bill and the impact he had on our team culture. He might not have been at the top of the org chart, but he sure knew how to build a high-functioning group. Bill understood people's strengths and built the team around them.

Now, you might be thinking, "Sure, that's great, but it sounds like he had a small department. I have a huge one."

My answer to that?

It doesn't matter.

The larger the department, the more you need a strong team of direct reports to help manage it. Which means you *still* start with a small group.

And yes—I said *start* with.

Bill showed it at the team level.

Roger, the CAO, showed it at the organizational level when he invited me to a roundtable discussion.

He didn't have to do that.

And I know I wasn't the only one invited. He was actively working to build connection with people deep in his organization. He welcomed their questions and perspectives.

Why?

Because he understood that as *the* leader, his decisions rippled across the whole organization. So he made time to connect with the people feeling those ripples.

Whether you know him personally or not, I think you'd agree—it's hard not to respect someone like that.

So if you have a large team, don't just hire or promote based on competence alone.

Hire people who reflect the kind of team culture you want to build. I know that is difficult and takes time, but spending that time up front pays off huge on the back end.

Because just like Bill created an environment where people thrived...
Another leader, with a different approach, could just as easily create one where people wither.

I could go on with anecdotes and examples, but the point is this:

You can shape the culture.

If you don't like the one you're in, define what you'd like it to become. It might take time—maybe a lot of it—but it's worth the effort.

The alternative? Letting things go "the way they've always been." And if that phrase makes your gut twist even a little? It should. That's a distinct signal for change.

Taking time to assess and build your culture isn't busywork.
It's improvement work.

Think of it this way: you're either training them to follow you, or you're training them to leave you. When you do the former, you're helping people grow — and the whole department, even the company, benefits. When it's the latter, you're teaching them how to thrive somewhere else.

When you build an environment for growth and innovation, you'll be glad you put in the time.

But what about the bigger picture? That's where culture comes in. Here are some questions to help you measure where you stand.

The Leadership Legacy You Build… and Leave

Culture isn't built in a day.
But it *is* built—through a series of intentional decisions, realizations, and interactions.

The truth is, it's cumulative.
Employees watch you the same way kids watch their parents: They follow what you do, not what you say.

Your communication, your reactions, your body language…
How you handle a curveball from an executive, how you treat people when the pressure's on.
They notice. They learn. And they remember.

The Camelot Effect

In my career, I recall only a couple times when everything felt like it was firing on all cylinders.
I've always called those moments *Camelot*. (cue the silver trumpets and angels singing)

That's when you've got the right team, rising leaders, and the processes in place to handle just about anything.
It feels effortless—but you know it isn't. Those moments don't last forever—but man, they're worth chasing.

What I didn't realize back then is how quickly Camelot can fade. Organizations shift. People get promoted or move on. Priorities change.

And before you know it, Camelot starts to break apart… brick by brick.

But I don't say that to discourage you.
I say it because it's worth it.

Every time we built Camelot, even for a short while, it mattered.
Its light echoes forward.
And knowing it *can* be built again? That's what keeps me going.

Culture isn't a destination.
It's a practice.

And the legacy you leave, whether you planned it or not, will live in the people who watched you lead.

Toolkit: Leadership Culture Check

You can't really go anywhere until you have a firm idea of where you are, or where you've been. The same thing goes with culture. Do I know what kind of culture my team would say we have?

- Is this culture mine—or did I inherit it?
- Who are my cultural carriers? Are they aligned with the tone I want to set?
- What kind of ripple effect do my comments or requests typically have?
- When was the last time I actively sought feedback from someone far removed from me on the org chart?
- Do I have at least one "Bill" on my team? Or better yet—am I that Bill?

I yours isn't where you want it to be... you have the reins.

Whether you act on it or not, the culture will reflect you.

Chapter 20: Inside-Out: Becoming Comfortable in Your Own Skin

There's something deeply disarming about people who are comfortable in their own skin. Not in an arrogant way—but in a real, grounded, human way. People who are willing to go first, who laugh at themselves, who don't need to dominate a room to be felt.

I didn't start out that way. In fact, I can pinpoint the exact moment things began to shift for me.

The Math Behind the Moment

I was in high school, sitting in English class, and we had one of those dreaded assignments where you had to read your essay or poem out loud. For years, I'd sit through those classes with rising anxiety, watching the clock, hoping I'd be saved by the bell.

Then one day, something shifted. The teacher asked, "Who would like to go first?"

And I just... raised my hand.

"I'll go."

It wasn't some sudden confidence breakthrough. I was just tired—tired of dreading it. The exhaustion finally outweighed the fear.

This was an English class, but my courage came from math. In a 45-minute period, if everyone spoke for 2–5 minutes, that was a lot of speeches. I figured most people would remember the *last* person before the bell, not the first. And my speech wasn't going to get any better while I stewed. So why not just get it over with?

Since then, I've gone first whenever I can. I didn't know it at the time, but I had started a process that would help me push past fear and become who I was meant to be. That may sound a bit melodramatic, but it's true.

That moment turned into a personal philosophy:

When in doubt, take the leap.

Go first.

Say hi.

Smile.

Not to dominate the room, but to set the tone—for myself and for how I want to be seen.

What started as a survival tactic for public speaking became a way to approach people. And when you're that comfortable in your own skin, it's contagious. People feel it. They relax. That's when connection becomes natural and easy.

Being disarming isn't some tactic to "work" someone. It's how you show up—genuinely. In a way that puts others at ease.

How to Practice Being Disarmingly You

The first step? Stop overthinking it. Once we get in our own heads, everything seems bigger and harder than it really is. I know—it's not as easy as it sounds. We're all our own worst enemy when it comes to self-deprecation and criticism. For me, this has probably taken a good ten years—but years well spent. Hopefully, you can make your realizations earlier and reduce that duration.

You can't outrun your own mind, so how do you shift its focus away from your flaws?

If your brain won't quit, distract it—pick a song, give it something else to focus on. Go back to when you were a little kid who simply said hi in the sandbox. You don't have to be fearless. You just have to try.

These little attempts, done regularly, build confidence over time.

Here are a few low-pressure ways to practice:

> **Toolkit: Disarming Training**

Smile. Even if you're not totally confident yet, a smile goes a long way. People naturally gravitate toward those who smile. It's a simple way to look friendly and open—as long as it's real. (No creepy smiles, please.)

Say hi. Keep it simple. You know your own name—start there. The hardest part is often just *starting*. Once you break the silence, the pressure fades.

Then look for something to compliment. Maybe it's a cool hairstyle or a sharp pair of shoes. If it's a work setting, start with context-based questions like:

- "Which company are you with?"
- "What brought you to the event?"
- "What do you enjoy most about your role?"

Ask what feels natural. That's what makes you come off as genuine—because you *are*.

Shake hands (if it's your thing). I'm a fan of a good handshake. Not too strong, not too limp—just confident. That said, this part's totally optional. Stick with what keeps you comfortable and culturally appropriate.

Know when to exit. If the conversation starts to lag—or you're feeling a bit overwhelmed—end it gracefully. A quick "It was great to meet you" and a polite exit does the job. You don't need to force magic in every interaction.

Comfort Builds Connection

Not every conversation will be amazing. And that's okay.

But just like anything else, the more you do it, the more natural it feels. And the more natural it feels, the better you'll get.

You don't need to master this overnight. Just go first, one small moment at a time. You don't even need to feel fully confident—just a little more than last time.

And yes, you'll stumble sometimes. That's part of it. So give yourself the grace and permission to fail.

Everything we've ever practiced a lot; we've gotten good at—it's true.

Stay on the path. Keep aiming for just a little better, and before long, you'll be better than you ever thought you could be.

If you want more low-pressure ways to practice, check out the Field Guide—I've tucked a bunch in there so you can pick and choose what works for you.

You don't need to be perfect. You just need to be present. Don't stress (or at least try not to) …you got this.

Chapter 21: Working Across Departments and Functions

One thing I've noticed in my career—and this may sound obvious—is this. People in different departments and functions have their own ways of communicating. It's a mix of jargon, acronyms, and their perceived place in the company hierarchy.

Inside their own group, it's just how they talk.

Comfortable.

Efficient.

It works for them.

The trouble is, if you're coming in from the outside, it can feel like going on vacation in a country where you don't speak the language. You might catch a few words you recognize, but most of it sails right over your head.

So that brings us to connection and language. Communicating in a way people truly understand is invaluable.

Language Study

Early in my career, I was as guilty as anyone. I started in Accounting and Finance, and anyone who's ever worked with those groups knows—we speak a little differently.

One big advantage of working in Finance was that we interacted with every group in the company. Whether you liked it or not (and let's be honest—most didn't), all departments operated within those wonderful financial constraints called budgets. For the technology folks I worked with, "budget" might as well have been a four-letter word. But I digress.

My job was to gather inputs, collect information, and consolidate the numbers so they met the requirements of my managers and executive leadership.

It didn't take long to notice most groups… well… didn't like Finance. Why? Because we tend to talk **at** people. We throw out words like "debits" and "credits" (Really—what the <bleep> is a debit?!), bring up limits no one knew existed, and when asked a question, the answer is almost always… "No."

It's like trying to buy an apple in another country where you don't understand the currency. They're telling you the price, you keep handing over bills, and you think you got it right—but you're never entirely sure.

That's Finance. As my career progressed and my responsibilities grew, I began to see that other groups had the same communication barriers—even within related areas. And the cost was real: lost time, wasted effort, and missed opportunities.

Most people just accept those barriers as part of the job.
I used to do the same—until I realized how much those invisible walls were slowing things down and wearing people out.

The more I saw it, the more I understood: if I wanted better results, I couldn't just operate in "finance mode" and expect others to adapt. I needed to meet them where they were, understand what mattered in their world, and connect the dots to mine.

That's when I stopped looking at Finance as just "my world" and started looking for ways to connect it to theirs.

In my experience, one big reason groups keep miscommunicating is simple: no one wants to go first. I get it, spending time getting to know another group isn't going to get that code written any faster or launch that email campaign any sooner. On the surface, it feels like non-value-added work. So if it's "not work," why do it?

Because it is work—and often more valuable in the long run. You still need to deliver your own results, but if you establish a relationship, a rapport, with a group you regularly work with, you'll almost always find you can understand requirements better and move faster than if you hadn't.

This doesn't mean entire departments have to go out for happy hour together or form a company bowling team (does anyone still do that?) Interdepartmental communication can improve dramatically with a single person making the effort. If no one makes the effort, it's no wonder you see the same arguments and obstacles year after year.

Change starts with one person.

So be that change.

I began looking at the communication gaps I'd noticed as a "language barrier." If I was going to be a true Finance partner, not just a number cruncher, I needed to recognize those languages and actually start learning them.

That's where the real magic happens—when both sides are willing to translate. Sometimes that means you sit and absorb their acronyms and processes until they finally make sense. Other times, it means you're the one breaking down your world into terms they can use.

And that's exactly how one of my favorite cross-functional wins started.

Warp Drives and Budget Forms – A Teaching Story

Every company has some sort of process, procedure, or red tape when groups request additional funds or resources. Ours was no different. We had the forms, no one liked them, and the process ranged from frustrating to downright painful. For us, they were the Statements of Work (SOWs) — requests that first went to Finance, and, if approved, moved up to executives for final sign-off.

At the time, I was working with a technology division. And let's just say Technology and Finance mix about as well as oil and water. For them, this process was about as close to hell on earth as they cared to get. Given all the rework and endless iterations these requests went through, it's no surprise they were frustrated and had little faith in the system. They'd send the forms, but you could tell they were already bracing for "No" before anyone even reviewed them.

I heard their stories and empathized. They were working hard, but they couldn't get what they needed to move projects forward.

From the Finance side, talking down highly frustrated people wasn't exactly a picnic either. The process wasn't going to change — this was corporate, and hell would freeze over before that happened. So if the system couldn't bend, what could I do to make it work better for them?

Then it hit me. The tech leaders spent a lot of time working these up before sending them to Finance — but what they really needed was guidance at the beginning of the process, so they didn't waste time. The problem was, I didn't always know who was working on a request unless they told me.

So I started providing guidance from the back end, reviewing their forms and setting up quick calls before they went up for approval. The biggest issue I saw was that while the tech folks were great at describing skill sets and requirements, many requests lacked a clear business justification — a key requirement on the form.

They knew exactly why they needed the resource; they just didn't know how to explain it in business terms.

So I changed my approach. If I couldn't follow the justification, I'd read it back to them and (depending on the audience) joke, "Right now this sounds like we need to realign impulse power through the warp conduit from Jeffries tube 16." That laugh broke the tension.

Then they'd say, "Well, basically it does this…" And I'd stop them right there.

"That's what you need to write. That's your justification. Once they can understand it, they'll see the importance of your request."

I also gave them one more tip: clearly state what would happen if they didn't get the resource. What would break? That gave executives a clear view of business risk in familiar terms.

The result? Fewer rejections, faster approvals, and tech leaders spending more time on their actual work and less time wrestling with forms.

I also offered to help them on the front-end next time — convinced that a 30-minute meeting could solve most of their issues before the form even went into the system.

That's when I realized: I wasn't just approving forms anymore — I was teaching..

By the time I'd worked through enough of those SOWs, something had shifted.

Helping tech leaders translate their requests into plain business language wasn't just improving approvals — it was building trust.

And that trust opened the door for me to see parts of their world I'd never had access to before.

I showed them I cared enough to help, and that created rapport. And rapport is just another word for connection.

Toolkit: Translation/Jargon Check

When you're working across teams, it's easy to fall into the trap of only speaking your own language. Here's a quick checklist I've learned the hard way to help you tell whether you're actually connecting—or just creating confusion:

- **Watch their faces/Observe body language** – Are you getting nods or blank stares? Blank stares = time to translate (I've never had that happen…. not).
- **Check the questions** – If all they ask is "What does that mean?" you might be in jargon mode. Worse still is no questions at all. Many people if they don't understand won't ask questions as they don't want to look dumb.
- **Flip the test** – Can they explain back your point in their words? If yes, you've landed it. Paraphrasing is not only useful, but clarifies understanding as well as being polite and courteous.
- **Balance the airtime** – If you're talking 90% of the time, you're probably not learning their language (By the way, this is hard for me… I like to talk).

The sooner you understand each other, the faster and more efficiently you'll work together—not just on this project, but the next ones too.

From Teaching to Learning

Teaching was only half the equation. If I wanted to truly connect across departments, I had to do the harder thing: learn their language too.

If I wanted to truly bridge the gap between Finance and other groups, I couldn't just help them speak my language—things like budgets (what we plan to spend), forecasts (what we think will actually happen), and optimization (how to stretch resources to get the best results). I had to be willing to learn theirs. In most cases, people aren't really going to be willing to truly learn your language, and I wouldn't blame them. I would never ask a tech person to take a finance course. But, over time, my tech partners started seeing things a bit differently. Some became excellent at business writing. Most recognized when they needed help and reached out. Just as teaching became a regular responsibility, learning was the next challenge. And like teaching, learning takes time, patience, and a willingness to feel a little lost at first.

The truth is, learning someone else's language is rarely urgent in the eyes of the business. It won't help you close this month's books any faster or make a project deadline magically move up. But in the long run, it can save you hours, reduce frustration, and turn "us versus them" into "we."

One of my biggest lessons in this came from working with the technology operations team at an entertainment company (yes, I worked with technology people a lot). At the time, we were in constant debate over cloud spending—basically, the costs of storing data and running systems on platforms like Amazon Web Services or Microsoft Azure. Endless meetings, repeated explanations, and very little progress. It was frustrating because our cloud spend was significant. The problem was that any idea or suggestion I had to help just hit a brick wall with a lot of blank looks. I knew I was missing something. They knew I was missing something. The only way forward was for me to stop pushing my agenda and start listening to theirs.

It also reminded me that translation works both ways. If teaching a little finance to Technology people could change our working relationship this much, what could learning their language do? That question set the stage for my next breakthrough — one that didn't happen over a Statement of Work form, but over months of patient back-and-forth.

Lost in the Cloud (and Finally Finding My Way Out) – A Learning Story

The SOW process taught me the power of translating someone else's work into terms another group could understand. But the reverse was also true — sometimes I needed to learn their language. And in this case, I definitely did.

In this company's technology platform, I was having a hard time understanding what the operations folks were doing and why certain cloud costs were so high. Spikes would occur at seemingly random times, making it nearly impossible to spot a pattern for modeling and forecasting. When I asked about it, we kept bumping heads in endless circular budget conversations that went nowhere.

So, I flipped the script. Instead of pushing my perspective, I sat down with them — literally, side by side — and started asking questions. I took notes, listened more than I talked, and never pretended to understand when I didn't.

It took months, but eventually the questions I was asking started to click with them. I still remember when one of the ops folks grinned and said, "Yeah, you're actually making sense now. You really are starting to understand what we're talking about."

That was a good feeling. Not because I suddenly knew everything (I certainly didn't), but because I was no longer on the outside looking in. The eye rolls when I came by stopped, and I was welcomed into the team's playful banter. I'd earned my stripes.

Over the next four years, we worked as true partners — finding ways to make things more efficient, cost-optimized, and better for the business. We saved millions of dollars and built trust that made future projects smoother from the start. Looking back, I'm convinced that learning their language opened the door to those great relationships. By the end of my time at the company, we'd gone from adversaries to trusted colleagues working toward the same goals.

One very important point I want you to notice: in neither of those cases — teaching or learning — did anyone come to me to start the process. If you invest the time and effort over years, that can happen, as it did with the technology leaders at that entertainment company. But it almost always starts with you. The teaching and learning began with me reaching out. Granted, I was in Finance, and I would never expect them to initiate, but as I said earlier, most people won't try to build rapport with another team. Whatever your role, if you truly want things to change, it's going to start with that person in the mirror.

When you take the time to learn someone else's language and help them learn yours, something shifts. It stops being "us" and "them" and starts being *we*.

And *we* can get a lot more done.

Chapter 22: The Power of Curiosity and Good Questions

In the last chapter, we talked about how asking questions can help solve problems and build understanding across teams.

But curiosity at work isn't just for fixing things.

It can build rapport before there's even an issue.

Asking questions about people and the work they do shows respect and a willingness to learn. That alone can lead to a stronger rapport with another team simply because you asked.

I've worked with technology people A LOT, but when I first joined the entertainment company, I was exposed to areas I'd never worked with directly — Legal, Business Operations, and Marketing.

The last one was a particular challenge for me. Finance craves predictability; Marketing thrived on chaos. That difference could have been a constant source of friction, but instead, I got curious about how they worked and why they made the choices they did.

Questions, Rapport, and Real Collaboration

When I took on working with Marketing, there were no major issues or emergencies to solve. My mandate was to build a solid working routine with the team so we could better understand what they planned to spend on, when those spends would happen, and — most importantly — how the previous spends actually performed.

The numbers were important—a vital part of the company's annual spend—but what I thought would be an easy setup turned into an education. As with all groups, Marketing had its own language—slang, shorthand, and, of course, acronyms. Being new to this, none of these made sense. I knew that in order to be effective in working with them, I'd need to build notes of terms and why they were important to Marketing. Now, I suppose I could have just forced them to a rigid spreadsheet process to get what I needed — I've seen people do that, but rapport is never created, only passive aggressive compliance.

So instead, I started asking questions — lots of them, and not to one member of the team, but to them all.

"What does this acronym stand for?"

"Why is this metric more important than that one?"

"How do you decide if a campaign was worth it?"

I kept a running list of their terms, definitions, and examples so I could start speaking in a way that made sense to them. Over time, those questions did more than fill my notebook — they showed the team I respected their expertise and wanted to understand their world, rather than audit it.

We ended up building a routine together, adjusting it as we went along. I'm not saying it was all peaches and roses, but because it worked from their point of view, the process was easier for them — and more productive for me. The information improved, the numbers became tighter, and the relationship became stronger.

I came to really enjoy talking and working with the entire Marketing team.

After several months, our relationships changed from the usual "Oh crap, Finance is coming" to genuine collaboration.

Curiosity and good questions, once again, saved the day.

The Role of Curiosity in Connection

Curiosity isn't just a way to pull information out of someone. You could use it that way, but when it's genuine, curiosity becomes an attitude—one built on interest and respect. And that attitude has a lasting impact, often well beyond the initial interaction.

What's great about curiosity at work is that it is common—even expected. If you ask a question that is on topic and are genuinely curious, no one will look at you sideways for it. In fact, questions like that showcase a person's want to learn and that in turn opens up more opportunities to build stronger relationships. Asking good questions shows someone that you value their experience and expertise.

In the workplace, nothing opens up communication like good solid questions. And that's where curiosity turns into connection—one conversation at a time.

Good Questions are Great Investments

Everyone already has more work than they can handle — how can questions possibly help when you're already backed up?

That is a very real concern. At work, it's best to look at questions as investments. They're not going to pay off immediately, but with a little extra, you can start to compile something significant.

Good questions clarify issues, increase knowledge, and build stronger connections. In a work environment, they also save the most valuable resource of all — time.

Take the story above with Marketing. The time we spent understanding each other didn't just reduce the time needed to get things done; it also improved efficiency and accuracy. That alone was worth the investment.

I can't claim to have worked with every type of team, but I firmly believe that asking questions—without demanding or judging—speeds up current tasks and makes future ones faster as well. And let's face it: it's far easier to work with people you like than with people you're constantly at odds with.

In my experience, that friction is rarely an all-out fight.
It's more like a slow, constant undercurrent of passive aggressiveness that drags everything down.
Because it's so constant, it often stops being recognized for what it is—it just becomes *normal*.

That's why good questions matter so much—they break through the *normal* and open up conversations that wouldn't happen otherwise.

Sometimes that means addressing tension between teams. Other times, it's about finding hidden opportunities.

Here's an example of one of the largest I was able to facilitate.

The Cloud's Silver Lining

Lost in the Cloud was just the beginning—getting my head around what was happening, what the costs were, how they were generated, and why they were needed. You've already heard that part. What you haven't heard is what happened next, because understanding the costs did not mean they magically went down.

It took more questions.

In one of those conversations, the Technology Operations (Ops) team mentioned that our cloud provider had been suggesting ways to save money for months.

That was exactly what I was looking for.

I knew I needed to meet those cloud representatives. The Ops team had no problem inviting them to come by so I could sit down with them.

The cloud representatives turned out to be personable, friendly, and easy to work with—I liked them right away. When I told them I wanted to see what opportunities we had to optimize and reduce our cloud spend. They smiled and said, "We are so glad to hear you say that! We've been wanting to work with your team for a while now."

That kicked off a process with the trifecta of Finance, Technology Ops, and the cloud reps. It wasn't fast, but in the end, we had a proposal for the CFO that would literally save the company millions.

Curiosity on the job can bring you connections—not just within your company, but with people and groups outside it. In this case, asking one more question linked me to the right people, built a new working relationship, and ultimately created an outcome none of us could have achieved alone.

Not every example of curiosity has to end with a multi-million-dollar savings. In fact, most don't. Sometimes, the best proof of how well good questions work is found in the small, everyday moments that build trust over time.

One of my favorites started small—but the payoff lasted much longer.

Early Morning Insights

Because of the distance to the office, I got into work early… I mean really early. Anyone who has had to deal with Los Angeles traffic can understand why I wanted to avoid the morning rush. Because of this, I would be the first Finance person in and one of only a handful of people in the entire building. One of my favorite things to do in those early hours was to take a walk of the floors and see who was around. Sometimes I got into unexpected conversations, sometimes not.

Of the people that were always in early, the tech Help Desk folks were always there. I got to know them very well (and honestly, not a bad group to stay on the good side of... just saying).

Occasionally, the help desk guys would ask me questions about the business—Why are we doing this? How come we're focused on that? The only times anyone outside of Finance talked numbers was usually in a once-a-quarter company meeting, and even then, the discussion was very high-level.

They were genuinely interested in what was going on. They had their opinions formed from their observations. Some were spot on. Some... not so much. Just by spending some time with them in the mornings, I was able to provide them with more insight into why and how things worked financially—budgets, which projects were prioritized, whether some business choices were good or bad—all part of their interests.

Eventually, I didn't even need to come over and chat—if they were curious, they found me. That's the thing about curiosity—it's contagious.

When you show genuine interest in others, they're far more likely to bring their own questions to you, and that's when real connection starts to stick.

Then you're not just connecting departments — you're connecting people.
And once people are connected, almost anything becomes easier to solve.

Here are some solid work questions to help you "break the ice" with other groups and show your interest.

Toolkit: Work Curiosity Icebreakers

Four High-Value Questions to Keep in Your Back Pocket:

- **Clarifying questions** – "Just to be sure I understand…" (Prevents mistakes before they happen.)
- **Interest questions** – "How does this work?" (Shows you value their knowledge)
- **Support questions** – "Is there anything I can take off your plate?" (Opens the door to collaboration.)
- **Perspective questions** – "How do you see the impact of this?" (Invites fresh ideas and context.)

Try one of these in your next conversation and watch how it shifts the tone.

Curiosity is one of the easiest ways to form connections—period. If you've got a genuine question about someone or what they do, ask it. The next time you're at work, don't just pass by your coworkers in the hall or nod at them in a meeting—stop, ask, and listen.

One question can change how you see your work, your team, even your career.

But you'll never find out—unless you ask.

Section IV: Leaving a Legacy

Legacy and connection don't often get mentioned in the same breath outside of family conversations.

But they belong together.

This section is about how you can leave your mark in a way that not only brightens your own day, but also creates a ripple of positivity for the people around you — whether they're close friends or strangers you may never meet again.

We'll explore how mentoring works in practice, and how to keep your connections strong over the long run. Because connection isn't just about today — it's about the story you leave behind, and ultimately, the story of your life.

Chapter 23: Connection as a Form of Legacy

The questions we ask can spark connection in the moment. But the way we show up—over and over—is what shapes how people remember us. Have you ever had someone ask you about a person and your response is something like, "Oh, Jim, he's a great guy"? Or maybe you've left a convenience store and thought to yourself, "That person was so nice." These are both situations that point to legacy. How you feel about someone after you're no longer in their presence *is* the legacy they passed onto you.

When we think of the word legacy, it usually conjures up thoughts of generations and things passed down over time. But at its core, legacy comes down to how you are remembered—and people remember how you made them feel.

That can be long-term impacts or just little moments in the course of a day.

Legacy in Everyday Moments

That big, generational legacy idea honestly feels kind of intimidating to me. I mean, that's a lot of pressure. I have to make sure that my life is this shining example to people decades from now? That's difficult to live up to for anyone. To me, legacy is the daily impact—the compliment you give, the smile you put on someone's face, the great feeling that sticks with them even after you leave the room.

Legacy doesn't have to be a warm fuzzy feeling. It can be wisdom or advice—something that changes how someone sees the world—simply from having interacted with you. One of the clearest examples of this kind of legacy came when I was working in a financial institution. The work was tough, and the politics were even tougher at my level. At the time, I worked closely with Theresa — she was in North Carolina, I was in California.

She told things straight—a rare quality—and one of those talks has stayed with me ever since.

Speaking Truth

Theresa was my controller, and we interacted constantly as I led Finance for the technology division. She had an infectious laugh, and our senses of humor were very similar…we hit it off immediately.

Those were frustrating times in my career. Being the person I am, I was far too open in how I spoke, which, at times, came back to bite me. Nothing really serious, but I realized that my tendency to trust people implicitly wasn't going to be an advantage in that environment.

Of course, Theresa and I talked about these situations. By then, we were definitely friends. One day, while I was venting about some office drama, she paused and said something that has stuck with me ever since:

"When people show you who they are, believe them."

At first, I'll admit, I didn't fully get it. But over time, I did. I started to pay closer attention to people's patterns, their consistency (or lack thereof), their responses under pressure, the way they treated others. I began to better observe human behavior to help me determine who I could really trust…and how far.

I still carry that concept with me today. It doesn't mean that I don't trust people, but I've gotten much better at evaluating who I want to spend my time with.

In short, I look for people who will make me better, as opposed to people who will just tell me what I want to hear. That way, I'm not only protecting my own energy, but also helping myself grow and be challenged.

That piece of professional wisdom from Theresa, that one short sentence, is a legacy I carry. It shaped me, guided me, and still helps me discern the quality of the connections I make today.

And it made me wonder—have I left that kind of impression on someone else? Honestly, I don't really know. Most people, as we mentioned before, don't really circle back and give you that kind of feedback. That, however, doesn't mean that your connection didn't make an impact. It's just that you probably won't know it.

If you're giving the best of yourself — genuinely and honestly — you don't need a payoff. For me, that's ok.

Connection isn't about what you get back—it's about what you give.

And speaking of giving…

The Glue that Binds Us

Have you ever encountered people who always seem to be the ones getting everyone together?

It could be dinners, outings, or just meeting at the local food truck. Even when they're not planning something, they somehow *fit* seamlessly into your social sphere.

I call these folks *glue people*.

They're not always the flashiest or the loudest in the room, but they're often at the center of the social web—keeping teams, groups, families, and sometimes even entire communities together.

Now, I'm not saying your legacy should be to become one of these people. You don't have to be the pillar of your community (yikes… the pressure…). What I *am* suggesting is that you can learn a lot by observing them, and then decide for yourself just how "sticky" you want to be.

I don't think being a glue person is binary. You're not either in or out like in a Clooney heist movie. I think it's something you grow into if you choose. And even the best glue people? Sometimes they need a break. It's not a job; in fact, it's a role that many take on without even realizing they're doing it.

One thing is certain: glue people understand the value of relationships. And they serve a vital role in keeping the rest of us connected.

You don't have to be that person all the time. Even for people like myself that gain energy from being around people, sometimes it is really nice to sit back and let someone else take the reins for a while.

And here's the fun part: there are different types of glue people. Let's take a look.

Active Glue

Growing up, my younger brother Bob and I fit the active role well. We had a great neighborhood full of kids our age, and sports was the clarion call that rallied everyone together. Summer meant wiffleball, pool games, or volleyball in our backyard under floodlights my dad set up. Winter meant turning the cul-de-sac into a snow-packed hockey rink. Whatever the season, Bob or I made the calls, and the neighborhood kids came running… literally.

That's what it looks like to be an active glue person. If no one's organizing, why not you? Back then it was picking up the phone; today it's sending a text or an invite. Sure, not everyone will show up every time. But they'll remember you as the one who cared enough to bring people together—and that matters.

Of course, as you get older with more responsibilities, it gets much harder to do what we did in the years of the endless summers. But just because you're not rallying the whole block doesn't mean it is less important, or noticed. In fact, most of my active glue moments are just setting up a coffee or grabbing lunch with someone. I've moved from groups to individuals. That's what I'm comfortable with now, but I still gain energy from larger groups as well.

I'm still in that active mode, but I've also found that the quiet, subtle planning can hit just as powerfully.

Secret Super Glue

That brings me to the people you might not even realize are glue people. One of our friends today is a perfect example. On first impression, she's not super outgoing—though she's warm, positive, and genuinely sweet. Since we've gotten to know her, she's been the spark behind most of our get-togethers, even the ones we couldn't attend.

She's not loud or pushy, but she's the one quietly planting the seeds. Whether it's a simple game night of dominoes, tossing out concert ideas, or making a night of it at a comedy club, she never forces it—her quiet suggestions just end up bringing folks together. Whether you can make it or not doesn't bother her a bit; you know another idea will be coming soon. It's a nice feeling.

And that's the thing: glue people, whether they realize it or not, create legacy. They are that steady but powerful force behind the shared memories, the new experiences, and the unexpected friendships. Whether it's a pick-up game of neighborhood basketball or a quiet evening of cards and laughter, these are the moments that build our friendships and deepen our connections.

Active or passive, these folks leave a legacy by creating memories—and shared memories form strong connections.

You don't have to be a glue person if it doesn't fit your personality or your season of life. Just take a moment to notice the glue people in your world and be grateful for the connections they help create.

So how do you create a legacy? Yep, you guessed it—connections. Every time you're connecting with someone—whether it's a brief chat, a work relationship, or the glue that holds a group together—you're stamping onto them the perception of you, for good or for ill.

Your legacy is yours to shape each day.

If you don't like the path it's on, you can always start again.

It isn't easy, but in the end, people remember the moments we gave them—not our money, titles, or accomplishments.

The memory of us is the ripple in the pond that keeps going.

And sometimes, it's not about the moments we create for many—it's about the impact we leave on one person at a time.

That's where mentorship becomes one of the most powerful forms of legacy.

Chapter 24: Mentorship and Long-Term Relationship Building

Mentoring

I think a lot of people get mentorship backwards. They believe the mentor is the one who chooses the person they're going to work with. I've even been in corporate-style programs where they *assign* you a mentor, forcing the relationship.

Both of those miss the mark, in my opinion. If anything, the old saying "When the student is ready, the master appears" is closer. Except I've never had someone mystically appear in my life in a puff of smoke and brimstone. Gandalf? Bueller?

My father taught me early on to look for mentors, because even though everyone says they're invaluable, they're surprisingly hard to find. Why?

Well first, no one has *"Mentor"* stamped on their office door. And second, because mentorship isn't something that's given, it's *earned*. A mentor is someone **you** pursue. *You* have to convince *them* that investing their time in you is worth it.

Even when you've earned a mentor, it doesn't mean the journey is going to be a piece of cake. A real mentor won't just tell you what you *want* to hear. They'll tell you what you *need* to hear, and chances are, you won't like it at first. That's the point. A good mentor challenges you to level up—not to coast.

In a strong mentoring relationship, you're also choosing to be accountable. You're taking the extra step of staying honest and showing your work until both of you feel like the journey has reached a natural pause—or it's time to move on to something else.

Now, if you're thinking, "Well, I've mentored lots of folks who worked for me," I have news for you: chances are, that wasn't mentorship (For those of you who actually were mentors...cheers to you). That was management, or maybe good teaching. If you did all the talking and guiding, and they just followed along, you weren't mentoring... you were instructing.

The opposite is true too. If you had a great boss who *felt* like a mentor, but you never asked tough questions or felt stretched, then you weren't being mentored either. You were just being led.

Management tells you what to do. Mentorship asks who you want to become.

I've had only a few mentors in my life. For this story, we're going to talk about Jim.

Rising above Revenge

Jim had run several successful companies, and I'd reached out to him for advice on how to build a business, something I thought I might pursue. He was a kind man with an easygoing way about him. It made him approachable and comfortable to talk with.

Then a situation erupted at work.

I'd found a mistake in the budget, something I probably should have caught earlier. As soon as I discovered it, I called corporate, owned up to the issue, and asked for a chance to correct it. The person I spoke with sympathized—but their window was closed.

Next stop: my manager's office. I explained what had happened, how it happened, and what I'd done to try and resolve it. He wasn't thrilled. He escalated it to the general manager.

And even though I was the one who found the mistake and worked to fix it, leadership decided there had to be consequences. I was demoted from my current position.

I was devastated. Embarrassed. On the verge of tears. By the time I got home and told my wife, that emotion had become rage. I was furious at what felt like a completely disproportionate punishment for an honest and admitted mistake.

My thoughts spiraled. My attitude soured. I stewed over how to "get even," which only made me angrier, especially as I realized how powerless I really was.

The smartest thing I did was call Jim.

I told him everything, and he listened—patiently, through all of my rage-filled venting. When I finally finished, he calmly shared his thoughts.

He reminded me that they didn't fire me, and that mattered. Then he told me, gently but directly, that my attitude (however justified it felt) wouldn't help me. In fact, it would only hurt me. It could give them further reason to question whether I belonged there at all.

I didn't want to hear it. But I listened.

Then he gave me the advice that changed everything:

He said "This is going to be very hard, but here's what I want you to do":

- Put your attitude and hurt feelings aside.
- Go back in there with the best attitude you can manage — even if you have to fake it.
- Work harder than you ever have before.
- Show them your worth. Show them they can't keep you down.

- Smile—literally—in the face of adversity.

So, I did.

It wasn't hard. It was *really* hard. But the more I faked a good attitude, the more it actually became real. I didn't complain. I stayed respectful. I worked hard and delivered.

Three months later, I was called into the general manager's office. I sat down and waited while he leaned back in his chair. (That wait? Also, quite hard.) Then he leaned forward, looked me in the eye, and said that, in retrospect, the demotion had probably been too harsh.

He told me that my work ethic, my output, and my attitude had changed their view. They were reinstating me to my original level.

And get this—three months after that—I was promoted.

Jim's advice didn't just save my career.
It helped me take care of my family.

It taught me how much attitude shapes outcomes.
And it reminded me that a true mentor doesn't just cheer you on, they challenge you to be better.

Mentorship isn't easy. We like to picture mentors as the wise guide on top of the mountain who always has the right words, or the cheerleader who sees your potential when you can't. Sometimes that's true. But the reality is, good mentors also challenge you. They hold up a mirror you may not want to face. They tell you what you *need* to hear, not what you *want* to hear.

That's what made Jim so effective. He didn't just sympathize with my frustration—he redirected it. And in the moment, it felt hard, even unfair. But the truth is, a mentor who only makes you feel good isn't really preparing you for growth.

Growth requires discomfort.

The best mentors are the ones willing to step into that uncomfortable space with you while you stay accountable to them.

The other side of this is equally important: if you want to *be* a mentor, you have to be willing to risk creating offense for the sake of the person's growth. It's not about scolding, or about being better than them. It's about caring enough to give honest, sometimes difficult guidance.

That's why mentorship matters so much—because when done well, it can change the trajectory of someone's career, or even their life.

Mentorship is just one kind of long-term relationship. But lasting connection goes far beyond career advice—it's about how we keep people in our lives once the initial spark fades.

Long Term Relationship Building

I think most people would agree it's easier to stay in contact with someone when you're geographically close. Maybe you check in with your parents, hang out with friends from high school, or grab a drink after work with colleagues. These interactions feel natural because you're consistently seeing the people you want to stay connected to.

But what happens when you're not? Life happens. People go to different schools, take jobs in other states, get married, have kids, change priorities. I'd bet most of us can still picture our old high school crew. And I'd also bet that, with a few exceptions, we've lost touch with most of them.

I think a big reason for that is when we're younger, we're still figuring ourselves out. We don't spend a lot of time thinking about who we want in our lives long-term. I know I didn't. That kind of clarity came much later for me.

Now, you might be thinking:

"Great, Marc. So you're saying all relationships fade?"

Not quite.

I'm saying that relationships you don't nurture are far more likely to fade.

And as we get older, the choice of who we keep in our lives becomes a lot more important.

One good example? That friend you can go years without talking to, but when you finally do, it feels like it was just yesterday. Cherish those. They're special.

When I was in my tweens and early teens, I'd ask my dad if I could go to a friend's house to hang out or play games. His answer was always the same:

"Do we know this child and their parents?"

If we didn't, the answer was no. As a kid, I just accepted it. But eventually I started to ask, "Why does that matter so much?"

My dad gave me a look—one of those serious-but-loving looks he had mastered—and said something that stuck with me.

"Because you are who you hang out with."

He explained that he didn't know how those other parents raised their kids, what kind of habits they had, or whether their home would be a good influence. He told me, "If you hang out with a group of smokers for a year, chances are, by the end of that year, you'll be smoking too."

At the time, I sort of got it. But the older I got, the more I understood. Peer pressure. The need to fit in. The power of habits and influence.

So how does this relate to long-term relationship building?

It starts with **choosing** the people you want to keep in your life... people who inspire you, challenge you, support you. People who make you better just by being who they are.

Once you've made that choice, then comes the harder part. How you maintain it when you may or may not actually see this person that often.

Time is the most precious resource we have, and as we get older, depending on our choices, we have far more demands on it.

It could be your career.
Your marriage
And the ultimate drain on time (and I mean this in the best possible way) ... your kids.

How do you keep up with people when you barely have time for yourself? We've talked about this in earlier chapters. The main thing about keeping up a long-term relationship is putting in the time.

If I've said anything in this book that's worth remembering, it's this:

Do what you're willing to do.

So if you're willing, here are some ways to start building that long-term structure.

Toolkit: Thinking Long Term

Trust me, small connections aren't small—because with long-term relationships, each one is like a brick. On its own it doesn't look like much, but brick by brick, you're building something that can last a lifetime.

Here are a few practical ways to stay connected:

1. **Start small** – Just check in on people. Text them. Message them on social media. Email. Make a quick phone call. The only way to go wrong is to not do anything at all.

2. **Be patient** – People are busy, just like you. You may not hear back quickly. This isn't about parity; it's about caring.

3. **Mark big moments** – Pay attention to birthdays, kids' birthdays, anniversaries, and even losses and struggles. Major life events are the ones that matter deeply to most people.

4. **Be genuine** – Reach out because you care and you're interested, not just to check a box.

Here's a close-to-home example from my own life.

Love Knows No Distance

I lived in my childhood home in Connecticut for 23 years—through college and for a few years afterward until I could afford to move out on my own. About five years later, I was living in California, 3,000 miles away. I've always been very close to my mother. When I lived at home, we talked all the time. After I moved away, I made it a point to still talk to her on the phone at least once a week.

Today, my mom texts me every single day (if I don't text her first). She tells me what she's up to, how she's doing, and that she loves me. We have a great relationship to this day. I haven't lived in Connecticut for almost 30 years, and yet my relationship with my mom is as strong as if I lived across the street.

Geography may seem like a good excuse, but technology has made it a weak one. Connection is more about will than about time.

Reaching out, even after a long while, shouldn't be embarrassing—the person on the other end is usually just happy to be remembered.

In fact, most of the people I've shared stories about in this book don't live anywhere near me. Chris, Kat, my mother, Jacob, the list goes on.

Yes, proximity can help a relationship grow faster. But that's mostly because it makes access easier. Even simple check-ins, spread out over time, can add up and build something lasting. It just takes longer.

I don't know about you, but spending time in staying connected with people I care about and am inspired by?

That's what I call an excellent investment.

Chapter 25: The Future Needs You: Connection in an AI World

At the time I'm writing this, AI is dominating the headlines—reshaping marketing, content, and entertainment. *"The future of work"* is everywhere.

Using AI

I use AI a lot in my consulting work, and even a little in this book. Mine even has a "personality" that cracks me up while it fixes my grammar, punctuation and long-winded sentences. It's tossed me some clever examples to help me get unstuck, but I mostly used those to spark my own stories and ideas.

I believe that using AI has helped me become a much better writer.

AI is fantastic at structure. But the content? That still has to come from the heart.

Now, I know what you're thinking: *Wait a minute...* It can write full-on stories with only a few prompts. What do you mean it can't do content?

Fair point. But when I say "content," I mean the truly human experience. AI can give a fair approximation, but that's all it is—an extrapolation of data and ideas. What it won't do is make up its own. You still have to do the prompting.

And if you still don't believe me.

Go ahead

Ask it.

Here's what mine said when I asked if it agreed with what I wrote above:

"Yes, this is an accurate way to describe the role of AI. AI excels at structure, grammar, and generating content that imitates human patterns. But the meaning, purpose, and emotional depth still come from humans. AI doesn't invent its own ideas; it responds to prompts and builds on existing data. It can approximate stories and style, but the lived experience, values, and personal perspective — those are uniquely human contributions."

So, much like Data from *Star Trek*, it agreed—in the longest way possible. 😊

And it proved my point.

AI doesn't really work well without an active human component—confirmed by AI itself.

What can AI do?

1. It's fast—much faster than any person at generating output.
2. It can analyze and manipulate large sets of data.
3. It's great at pattern recognition and repetition.

But here's where it stops short.

What can't AI do?

1. It doesn't start anything—it needs human purpose and direction.
2. It can't supply imagination, values, or context for what matters.
3. It can't be you. It can fake faces and voices, but not the *real you*—your quirks, your values, your humanity.

I know that that's not the full list of what AI can and can't do, but you get the idea.

And like most new things with humans, the unknown can be frightening. Technology moves so fast these days that it's tough to keep up—let alone really understand what's going on.

I can honestly say I'm not scared of AI or its potential. I see it as an excellent tool—one that can help us maximize our own. And like it or not, it's here to stay. So, we'd better learn how to live with it—and live well.

As a tool, AI is changing how we work, what tools we use, and how we navigate everyday life. But what it won't do is give us the feeling of community and connection.

Think of the pandemic. That was life without connection—and I'm in no hurry to go back. People need people. Shared experience is part of who we are. We crave the energy of a great concert. The infectious laughter in a comedy club. These moments will never go out of style. AI can't create or replace that for us.

As AI becomes more embedded in our daily lives, I've been thinking about what makes us distinctly human—and how we protect that in a world of super-accelerating technology.

Being Known

The answer? We lean **heavily** into our humanity and we make ourselves known.

In short, we strive for: *personhood.*

What do I mean by that? In this context, personhood is the state of being known—really known—by enough people that you become harder to fake.

Think about it: a video surfaces showing you saying something completely out of character. If someone doesn't know you, they might believe it. But the people who do know you? They'd see through it immediately.

Why? Because they know your values. They know your heart. They know the real you.

And in a world where fakes can be convincing, your personhood, your humanity becomes your strongest defense.

That might sound a little scary, but here's the upside:

In a digital world, you don't need more technology to defend your humanity. You just need to be you—consistently, openly, and visibly—with other humans.

What does that even look like? It means doing things that have nothing to do with a screen. Like writing a little "I love you" note on the grocery list for your partner. Or cracking a joke that makes a stranger smile in line at the store.

As advanced as AI becomes, it still can't do that.

It has a vast pool of knowledge. It can solve complex problems. It has intelligence—sure.
But emotional intelligence?

You can't just plug and play that.

And yes, tech folks—I know plug-and-play is one of technology's biggest myths.

Humans have always been tribal. We seek belonging. We thrive in community.

That's why being a connector—someone who sees, hears, and values others—will be a superpower in a world leaning toward automation.

Think about it: who's the more valuable employee?

The one who's technically brilliant?

Or the one who can teach, manage, and motivate a group of brilliant people to accomplish something extraordinary?

That second person might not be the best at the tech itself, but they know how to connect. They know how to **lead**.

And that is an irreplaceable talent in every kind of organization.

That's why I believe the future isn't about resisting AI, it's about **partnering with it** in a way that amplifies the best parts of being human.

The warmth.

The care.

The follow-through.

AI can help you show up, but it can't *be* you.

That truth, that AI can't replace you, is huge. It won't teach your kids manners, right and wrong, or how to treat people. They learn that from you. From what you say, sure, but if you're a parent, then you know full well that kids do as you do WAY more than they do as you say.

Being an Active Member of Humanity

I've heard it said that kids spell love T-I-M-E. I don't know who made that up, but it is as brilliant as it is true. Kids remember that you were there at that baseball game or Shakespeare production. They remember that you showed up—and that's connection at its most fundamental level.

And here's the thing: it isn't just kids; adults feel the same way. Time and attention still speak the loudest. It is the time and attention that we spread from ourselves that shows people that they are important to us. The funny thing is, in a world changing at breakneck speed, our advantage may be the parts of us that *don't* change—love, grief, laughter, encouragement, achievement. Those are part of the human condition, and they will not be replaced by a hotfix or a new version.

AI can't make this part of life better for you. It won't enjoy that concert, cheer with you for your team, or enjoy that shared cup of coffee with a friend.

You can't outsource happiness any more than you can automate it.

Our actions, encouragement, and small efforts are more meaningful not because of their regularity, but because they show that we took the time to think about that person—and then do something about it.

You don't need to be an expert in AI to shape the future. You don't even have to use it or pay attention to it. You just need to be someone people can count on. Someone who shows up. Someone who listens, encourages, and leads by example.

Because in a world where so much is being automated, **what you do by choice becomes your legacy**.

How you treat people.

How you make them feel.

How they remember you after you're not there.

What you show your kids and your coworkers and your friends matters, because you're sharing your thoughts, feelings, and who you truly are.

So let me ask you something:

What do you want to be remembered for?

Being Memorable

As we talked about with legacy, this doesn't have to mean what future generations remember. I'm talking about the people you talk to this week, or next month, and over the next year.

Will people say that you were present, that you made a difference in their day? That you made time for people?

Will they recall that you reached out, followed up, and gave people the sense that they mattered?

That you connected?

The world is moving fast and may never slow down. But the people in your life? They're still people. And that means the most important opportunities to connect will never come from your calendar.

They'll come from your willingness to reach out and engage.

Connection may feel old-fashioned, but it isn't. It's the most future-proof thing we can do.

The future doesn't just need AI.

The future needs you.

Your presence.
Your empathy.
Your ability to make someone feel seen.

Stay human.
Stay connected.
The future is waiting.

Conclusion

Well, here we are. Unless you're one of those friends of mine who reads the last chapter of a book first, you've made it all the way through.

It is my sincerest wish that in this *grocery store* of observations, stories, and examples, you found something useful — or, more importantly, that your desire for connection has been kindled.

I believe we're all better when we're together — sharing our joys, our sorrows, and the everyday paths of life.

Connection doesn't require perfection or extra time. It can fit naturally into your schedule, because we all have some downtime. What better way to use it than by keeping your relationships alive and blooming?

And you don't need to be an extrovert. Connection isn't about personality type — it's about choosing to act. A text, a thank-you, a smile, a story. Small things, done consistently, are what matter.

If you take anything away from this book, let it be that change starts with action, no matter how small. Progress is progress. Wherever you're comfortable, start there — and let it grow.

When we reach out, we show our caring — and the world needs more of that. We're not meant to be insular or isolated. We need people.

Thank you for spending your time with me. Now close this book, and go say hello to someone.

I hope I run into you somewhere down the road.

Sincerely,

Marc Zawrotny

P.S. – If you'd like to keep the conversation going, just feel free to Reach Out. I'd truly love to hear from you. 😊

The Connector's Field Guide

This Field Guide gathers the best connection practices into one quick-access place. It's organized into five parts — Grounding, Getting Started, Building Consistency, At Work, and Legacy — so you can flip straight to the section you need. Along the way, you'll also find more options and stories to help you build habits that fit your personality. Think of it like a grocery store: take what you want, leave the rest, and work with what fits you best.

Table of Contents

Grounding Yourself 187
Naming and Processing Emotions 187
EQ Workouts for Real Life 188

Getting Started 190
Low-Effort Starters 190
Medium-Energy Builders 191
Deeper Connection Moves 192
Active and Passive Connecting 192
Gotta Use Your Tools 194
Putting Your Tools to Work 196
Low-Energy Ways to Stay Connected 197

Building Consistency 198
Determine who you want to connect more with. 198
Find a cadence that feels doable 199
Use tools to help. 200
Figure out when and where you're most comfortable reaching out. 200
Following Up 201
Keeping Respect 201
5 Follow-Up Texts That Don't Feel Pushy 202
How to Use What's Already There (Opportunities) 203
Quick Responses That Still Show You Care 205

At Work 207

Keys to Working With Your Boss 207
    Keys to Working With Admins 208
    Leadership Culture Check 208
    Respectful Responding 209
    Let them Save Face 210
    Questions to Find Common Ground 211
    Translation/Jargon Check 211
    Storytelling 101 212
    The Secret Door Isn't Just for Starters 213

Legacy 215
    Thinking Long Term 215
    Water Your Network, Even When Nothing's Growing 215
    Keeping Your Network Flourishing 216
    Reconnecting Years Later 217
    The Legacy You Don't Intend to Leave 218
    Paying It Forward 218

Grounding Yourself

You've probably heard ideas like this before. Regardless, how you control your own actions and reactions to things shows up in every relationship you have. You likely already have a set of practices you use, though often unconsciously rather than actively. Grounding yourself means noticing those practices and bringing them to the surface. That way, you can use them with intention — putting the best of yourself into your interactions. As you become more aware of yourself, remember that others are picking up on you too.

Our brains are amazing supercomputers that notice micro-reactions in facial movements, body language, and even tone of voice. Have you ever been bothered by something, but someone asks "Hey, are you alright?" even though you never said anything? I'll bet you have. People pick up on emotions and it becomes the baseline for your interaction even before you've opened your mouth.

So, if you want to connect well with others, you have to be steady with yourself. That means making sure you're not taking out something unrelated on someone else **and** looking at your emotions, reactions, and state of mind so you can be fully engaged instead of running on autopilot. This is where "grounding" comes in. Think of it like taking that big deep breath before a performance or a speech. It clears your head so you can put your best foot forward.

Naming and Processing Emotions

One of the most impactful ways to grow emotional intelligence is to get better at identifying and working with your emotions instead of suppressing or reacting. Use this step-by-step to build the habit:

- **Pause and notice** – Check what you're feeling physically. What's your first urge? If you've got that

nervous feeling or are just not feeling 100%, acknowledge that.
- **Ask yourself what you're actually feeling** – Go beyond just "angry" or "sad." When I've been in a mood, and people ask what's wrong, I often admit I don't know — but hope to figure it out soon. Naming a feeling helps to resolve those negative ones.
- **Name it** – Say it out loud or write it down. It could be 'I feel dismissed,' or 'I feel anxious.' Most of the time, I tend to write this down on paper or on the computer. For saying it out loud, the car is the perfect place. Getting it "out of your own head" does wonders.
- **Validate it** – Remind yourself it's okay to feel this way – 'It's okay to feel this way.' This is really hard. We are our own worst critics and tend to dwell on feelings. Forgiving yourself— Even just giving yourself a break can be freeing.
- **Look for the message** – Examine the need or value underneath. The "ask" questions above are to help you really analyze the problem. Once identified, you'll find that the solution presents itself.
- **Choose a thoughtful response** – Decide what action you'll take. Many times, I thought I was going to chew someone out when the time came. That three seconds of satisfaction isn't worth it. I inevitably find a more reasonable and calmer way to engage even if my emotions are running high.

This practice isn't about perfection. It's about paying attention, staying curious, and being kinder to yourself in the process.

EQ Workouts for Real Life

I'm not an expert on emotional intelligence. What I can share are a few small things I do that help me show up better in conversations and connections. Think of these as little "reps" you can try out in everyday life.

- **Pause before reacting** – If a message irritates me, I take five seconds before I respond. It saves me from saying something I regret. (Especially with electronic mediums — those don't ever really go away)
- **Ask one more question** – I try to follow up with curiosity — it shows I care and usually uncovers more than I expected. Questions are the beginning of knowledge and therefore connection.
- **Summarize before responding** – Repeating back what someone said ("So what I'm hearing is…") helps them feel understood. I've found this to be an invaluable tool to prevent a cascade of misunderstanding.
- **Send a quick thank-you** – Gratitude goes a long way, and it doesn't take much effort. It costs you nothing to do, and it could be worth a treasure to the recipient.
- **Check in with myself** – Once a week I ask: "What's been driving my mood this week?" It helps me reset before it leaks into my relationships. Sometimes… you just don't have it. And that's okay. Knowing where you stand helps keep you from putting yourself into a bad situation unintentionally.

I'm not perfect at any of these, but I've found they make me a little better day by day — and that's what matters.

Once you've grounded yourself and brought your best forward, the next step is simple: get started.

Getting Started

Just starting out is the hardest part—especially if you're not naturally someone who reaches out. The key is to take things slowly and only do what you're actually willing to do. This is your journey, not anyone else's. And remember, this isn't a checklist where you 'do these things and suddenly you're a connector.' No such list exists. Take what fits, leave what doesn't.

Whatever you can commit to consistently is the right place to start. There's no gold standard here, no "minimum bar" you have to clear. The goal is to pick something small, doable, and repeatable. Over time, that consistency builds confidence.

Think of this section like a training plan—you don't start by lifting the heaviest weight, you start with what you can actually handle. Connection works the same way. These ideas scale from light to heavier lifts, so you can pick what works today and build from there.

Low-Effort Starters

These are the simplest methods. They take almost no energy, but over time they build confidence. That's key, because simple isn't always easy.

- **Send a text** – Try a quick "Hey, was thinking about you" text per week (or per month if that's more realistic).
- **Keep a running list** – Track "people I like/want to stay connected with" in your Notes app or even on paper if it suits you. When someone crosses your mind, add them. That list becomes your go-to roster for check-ins.
- **Thank by name** – At the end of meetings or casual conversations, thank someone by name (and smile!). Names

are powerful—if you're not sure how to pronounce one, just ask. People appreciate it.
- **Say hi** – Make it a habit to simply say hello to people—in the grocery store, at the gym, wherever. Even that small gesture builds confidence.
- **Smile** – It's contagious, and it makes others more likely to engage with you. Remember to be genuine, otherwise you come off kinda creepy.

Medium-Energy Builders

Once the lower-effort steps feel natural, you can start to build the habit a bit more. Your confidence should be in a place where these don't feel difficult. If they still do, stick with the low-effort ones. This isn't a race—it's just about improving a little over time.

- **Set reminders** – Put one on your calendar each week labeled "Reach Out." No guilt… just a nudge. You don't even need to put in a name if you're not sure — just build the habit.
- **Send a memory ping** – Share a moment you both remember. *"This popped into my head today — remember when we…"* (people love shared nostalgia. I do this one ALL the time).
- **Rotate seats** – Change up who you sit with at lunch or in meetings. You'd be surprised how easily we slip into the pattern of the same seats and the same people. Shake it up.
- **Comment meaningfully** – Go beyond a like. Be supportive on a friend's post and let them feel seen. Comments take effort — and people notice that.
- **Start your own mini-coffee club** – Meet one person per month (virtual counts too!). And notice I didn't say one new person — reconnecting often builds friendships.
- **Take extra time** – At work or social events, spend a little longer talking with someone you don't know—even just to introduce yourself. This can be intimidating, but it will certainly boost your confidence.

- **Offer help** – Give a helping hand when you see the opportunity. It could be as simple as holding a door open or grabbing a product from a high shelf.

Deeper Connection Moves

Here's where connection goes from casual to meaningful. It takes more effort—but the payoff is stronger relationships. You should feel the difference in these interactions; they're not just about reaching out; they're about really connecting.

- **Offer appreciation** – Give a genuine "I appreciate you" for something small, but meaningful. Don't wait for big moments — appreciation hits hardest in the ordinary.
- **Ask for advice** – People love being valued for their expertise — it gives them a chance to be helpful.
- **Share something personal** – Keep it small, like a book you're reading or a challenge you're working on. Vulnerability signals trust and deepens connection.
- **Write a letter** – Send someone a real letter or card. It doesn't have to be long. The effort and the gesture alone stand out. (Cursive still earns bonus points — provided they can read it 😊)
- **Own the drift** – Pick someone you've drifted from and reconnect. "Hey, I know it's been a while. Would love to catch up." You'd be surprised how often people are happy to hear from you.
- **Ask better questions** – Instead of "How's work?" try "What's been challenging you lately?" or "What's bringing you joy right now?" You'll get far better answers than 'Fine.'

Active and Passive Connecting

Some connections happen face-to-face. Others happen from the couch. Both count. Don't think you're "not doing anything" if you pick a lower-energy method—connection is connection.

Getting off the couch

Sometimes you find yourself in that rut: go to work, come home, eat, turn on the TV, repeat. Change it up. Get out of the house, share some laughs, do something different—you'll feel better for it.

- **Grab a quick drink (Low)** – Coffee, tea, or a bar drink with a friend. A chance to talk about the day, vent, or just catch up. These usually last only as long as the drink, so the time is completely up to you.
- **Make get-together plans (Low–Med)** – Invite folks over (excellent excuse to tidy up the house…), host a game night with snacks, or head out for dinner or an event.
- **Plan regular outings (Med)** – Think date nights, movie outings, or trying new restaurants. I know people who make it a goal to never repeat a restaurant, which takes planning—but that's also where the fun is.
- **Create regular events (Med–High)** – Poker nights, local D&D (Yes, I mean Dungeons and Dragons), coffee clubs. These take more coordination and energy—especially with bigger groups—but the payoff is also bigger.

Connections from the couch

On the flip side, sometimes you just feel like hanging in—or maybe you've got a few spare minutes while waiting for food to cook. Connection doesn't have to take a lot of energy.

- **Send a text (Low)** – A simple "Checking in on you" or "Was thinking of you, hope you're doing alright."
- **Make a quick call (Low)** – Much like the text. If you get voicemail, leave a short message. If you connect, use it to set up time for coffee or a beer.
- **Set up an online call (Medium)** – Takes a little coordination, but you can set up regular check-ins. My wife

uses this very effectively with some of her friends in California as they'll set up virtual Happy Hours.
- **Plan a scheduled online activity (Medium–High)** – A little more work since you're juggling schedules, but worth it. During the pandemic, I set up online poker games. It gave people a chance to laugh, talk, and connect.

Whether you're connecting in person or from the couch, the point is the same: use what you already have — especially the tools in your pocket.

Gotta Use Your Tools

You've got more ways to connect than ever before—it's just a matter of actually using them. The trick is to turn the everyday stuff (phones, apps, downtime) into little nudges for connection instead of letting them slip by.

We've all got the tools, but the question is: what's the best way to use them? It depends on you, but there are some realistic "rules of the road" that help you choose the right method and use it well.

Phone Calls

Yes, people still do this. If you hit that dreaded "voicemail not set up," that's probably your clue to try another way. If you do call, keep these in mind so you respect the other person's time:

- **Keep voicemails under a minute** – Most people are busy. Even if it's just a check-in, be brief.
- **Ask if they have time to talk** – Lots of people answer mid-task. Give them the chance to bow out politely.

- **Check on time** – If you've got a long story, ask whether now's the moment. Sometimes it's better saved for later.

Texting

You'll probably use this most. Everyone has their own style, but here are a few good rules to keep in mind.

- **Use short, genuine check-ins** – *"Thinking of you"* works wonders. Long blocks of texts these days are mostly ignored. If you have that much to say, consider calling.
- **Sarcasm/Jokes** – Skip these unless you're sure they'll land. Unless you know someone *really* well, tone can backfire at the speed of light.
- **Don't overdo it** – Daily texts can slide from "thoughtful" to "annoying" (or worse... creepy).

Social Media

This is where the younger crowd tends to live and shine. From posts to DMs to video messages, it's their main medium. The key is to remember that posts — like texts — can be taken out of context, so being intentional goes a long way.

- **Be thoughtful with posting** – Never post about someone without their knowledge—or anything you wouldn't say to them directly. The internet never forgets.
- **Use direct messages for connection** – DMs feel more personal than a public post, but they still follow text rules—best with people you already know.
- **Practice patience** – People use apps differently, and platforms move at different speeds. A delay doesn't mean disinterest.

Email

Not always the flashiest option, but useful in the right situations. Email works best when:

- **Finding them** – It's the only contact info you have.
- **Driving business** – You're reaching out to work or business connections who are used to checking email.
- **Build long-term connections** – You want something with a bit more permanence (longer updates, thoughtful notes). It works both to establish new connections and to strengthen existing ones.

Remember that the ways to connect may not always sync with how you like to. I think the relationship definitely outweighs the discomfort.

Different people, different channels. The key isn't picking the "right" one every time — it's making the most of the tools you already have. Let's look at some simple ways to do that.

Putting Your Tools to Work

Below are a few simple ways to cut out the indecision and actually keep up with people:

- **Try an alphabet scroll** – Stuck on who to reach out to? Open your contacts, pick a letter, and send a quick hello to the first name that jumps out. *(This is my personal favorite.)*
- **Set reminders** – Birthdays, anniversaries, or just a "ping Joe" on your calendar. A little prompt goes a long way.
- **Make drive-time calls** – If you've got a commute or a long stretch of road time, use it (hands-free, of course) to catch up with someone. A long drive feels shorter—and a lot more enjoyable—when you're talking to a friend.

Sometimes the simplest gestures carry the most weight. If you're low on energy, here are quick, low-effort ways to stay in touch.

Low-Energy Ways to Stay Connected

Not all connection needs to be on the phone or through long texts. Social media and small gestures count too — especially for younger generations who often use those platforms as their primary way of keeping up. (That's not a slight, just an acknowledgement that we all communicate differently.)

Here are a few easy, low-effort ways to stay connected:

- **Share humor** – A meme or funny video (no context needed).
- **React meaningfully** – Drop a "like" or a short comment on someone's post.
- **Forward articles** – Send something interesting with: "Thought of you — this made me smile."
- **Send a voice memo** – A quick recording instead of typing.
- **Set recurring reminders** – Ping one person per week to keep the habit alive. Just don't lean on this too much: a meme once in a while is fun, but being "meme'd to death" gets old fast.

As always, know your audience. These may be low-energy connectors, but you don't want them to come across as low-caring.

Building Consistency

This is where the rubber meets the road. It all starts with the will to begin, and to hold yourself accountable to the rules that you set. Remember, you're not doing this for anyone else. The only judgment is your own, so make sure that you set goals you can easily reach.

Determine who you want to connect more with.

Often the hardest part is just figuring out who. Here are some categories to jog your memory:

- **Neighbors** – Do you have neighbors you'd like to know better? Having good neighbors never hurts.
- **Gym / Fitness** – You start noticing the same people at the same times. Saying hi can make workouts a lot more fun.
- **Family** – Life takes people in different directions. Is there a family member you'd like to reconnect with?
- **Work Colleagues** – Someone in your department (or outside of it) you'd like to learn from or build with?
- **Old Acquaintances** – People come and go in our lives. Who would you like to check back in with?
- **Mentors / Role Models** – Someone you admire who might be open to a conversation.
- **Friends of Friends** – That person you met once at a barbecue or wedding and thought, "I'd like to know them better."
- **Classmates / Alumni** – Old school or college friends, or alumni networks where you already share a bond.

- **Community Connections** – Fellow parents at your kid's school, people from church, a book club, or volunteer group.
- **Online Connections** – Someone you interact with on LinkedIn, Instagram, or another platform who feels like more than just a casual follow.

Remember, there are no wrong choices. If you want to connect with others, the important part is just beginning.

Find a cadence that feels doable.

You'll only do things consistently if they feel reasonable to you. This isn't about forcing yourself out of your comfort zone—it's about finding a rhythm that works. Connection should feel like a natural part of life, not one more task on a to-do list.

- **Start slow** – Consistency counts more than quantity.
  - **Once a month** – Easy to schedule, low energy.
  - **Once a week** – Still low energy, but requires some awareness.
  - **Daily** – I'll be honest: this one's heroic. I consider myself pretty active when it comes to connecting, and even I don't do this.
  - **Now and then** – Use tools to help keep you on track, because it's easy to forget.
- **Be okay with your choice** – One or two check-ins a month may feel like nothing—but it's something. And something is always better than nothing.
- **Increase when comfortable** – Think of this as training for the long haul, not a short-term goal. You decide how much and when. Stick with what works, and only add more if you want to.

I want to reiterate: this book isn't about becoming a social butterfly if that's not who you are. It's for anyone who wants to connect more with people, in whatever way works best for them. We're all different, and hopefully, we're all growing.

Use tools to help.

We talked about phones earlier, but since we're talking cadence, it's worth reiterating: your tools matter—and not all of them are phones.

- **Use your phone** – You carry them everywhere anyway, so let them be more useful than just playing games.
    - **Set reminders** – Let your phone do the remembering for you.
    - **Use alarms** – If you need more than the visual cue, let your phone annoy you into action. 😉
- **Mark a wall calendar** – Write notes or reminders where you'll see them daily. It's harder to ignore something staring you in the face.
- **Post sticky notes** – Put them everywhere: bathroom mirror, computer screen, rearview mirror. If you can't miss it, it works.

Habits are difficult to build and just as difficult to break. Do whatever makes the process easiest for you. I've used—and still use—all of these.

Figure out when and where you're most comfortable reaching out.

The best times to connect are the ones that fit seamlessly into your schedule. I don't tend to stick to one set time, but I almost always use my car time. After braving California traffic for years, it was practically a lifesaver.

When

- **Morning** – If you're a morning person with energy before the day kicks in, use it. Just read your audience—some folks aren't ready to connect before coffee.

- **Afternoon** – Everyone needs a break sometimes. Step away from your desk, send a quick text, or chat with someone nearby.
- **Evening** – Best done before you fully settle in for the night. You can connect from the couch, but sometimes it's just time to chill.

Where

- **Home** – Comfortable and familiar, best for family, close friends, or long distance.
- **Car** – My personal favorite. Hands-free calls or quick texts (voice-to-text) can turn a commute into something enjoyable. Making traffic feel better? That's a win.
- **Office** – Naturally geared toward colleagues and work friends. Keep it professional, but don't miss the small chances to connect.

I know I'm repeating myself, but the point is simple: build connection into the life you already live. Connection is easier when it becomes part of what you already do, not another chore on the list.

Following Up

This seems like this would be an important section. How come there's no tips or tricks? Because when you break it down, following up is simply connecting again — but with intention. Whatever you used to help you start is exactly what you'll use to keep it going.

Keeping Respect

The best thing you can do is to remember to respect the other person's time and where they're at right now.

- **Detach from results** – A lack of reply doesn't erase the value of your effort. The joy is in the giving, not the receiving.

- **Keep it simple** – A kind word or quick check-in is enough. I find the longer the message you leave, the more you expect a reply. Short and genuine makes it easier for both of you.
- **Honor the silence** – Sometimes people just aren't ready, or they're simply not communicative in the same way you are. That doesn't mean you stop caring — it just means your care shows up without strings attached.
- **Respect the lane** – Some people respond to texts but ignore email, or reply on social but not by phone. If you know their preferred channel, use it. Meet them where they are instead of forcing them into yours.
- **Respect yourself** – Consider your time and energy. If you've invested in someone who never responds, decide when it's healthier to put that energy elsewhere. Protecting your energy is vital for your own health and your other relationships.

Sometimes silence is the answer you get — and that's okay. You'll never go wrong if you keep respect front and center.

Speaking of respect, not being pushy is a good place to start. Here are some easy suggestions to use.

5 Follow-Up Texts That Don't Feel Pushy

Sometimes you want to check in without making it feel like an obligation or a test. Here are five simple texts you can use (or adapt) that keep the tone light, caring, and no-pressure:

1. **"Checking in — hope you're well."**
   Straightforward and genuine. It shows you care without asking for anything back.
2. **"Was thinking of you recently. Hope you're having a good day."**
   A little more personal. Just letting someone know they crossed your mind.
3. **"Happy Friday!"**
   Simple, cheerful, and universal. Fridays are a natural bright spot.

4. **"Have a great day, [Name]."**
   Short, upbeat, and energizing. Send this when you're in a good mood — that energy comes through.
5. **"Hey [Name], sending good thoughts to you."**
   Especially powerful if you know someone is going through a tough time. Even from a distance, they'll feel your support.

Feel free to embellish these to your style (emojis, memes, etc.) — just keep it from being over the top. None of these expect a reply. They land as small, kind reminders that you're in their corner.

How to Use What's Already There (Opportunities)

Finding that time

Once you've decided to start, you've cleared the hardest hurdle. As I mentioned in the book, there are countless moments in the day that most people don't recognize as opportunities. They're things you already do almost every day without a second thought.

The key is to notice them — and use them. That way, connection doesn't feel like one more chore on your list. It simply becomes part of your life as it already exists.

As I talked about in *Don't Waste the Wait*, a lot of connection opportunities are already baked into your day. Waiting in line, driving across town, sitting in a lobby — all of these can be connection moments if you decide to use them.

You don't need to carve out new hours. You just need to notice the minutes you already have and put them to work.

Small Gestures

Whatever you choose, keep it natural and authentic to you.

- Text someone "This made me think of you" with a funny meme or article
- Offer a sincere compliment—no strings attached
- Ask someone's name (then actually remember it)
- Say "Good job" in front of their boss
- Bring an extra coffee to a coworker
- Share a helpful link with no ask
- Mention something positive they said… weeks later
- Offer your seat
- Send a birthday text
- Let someone vent without fixing it (yes men… I'm talking to **you**)
- Say "thank you" to someone who usually gets ignored

Don't Waste the Wait

In the car

Whether your commute is 10 minutes or an hour, you've got choices. I used to have a one-hour commute to work one way. You either find something to do with that time, or you start building a nice pot of road rage. So, what can you do?

- Listen to music
- Listen to podcasts/audible books
- Make some calls (Make sure you have a hands-free way of doing this please. I don't want anyone getting a ticket while they're connecting.)

In the gym – Interactions

- **The front desk** – a cheerful smile and a hello is a great way to help someone else's day as well as yourself.

- **Spot someone** – This is situational, but if someone needs help, be that person. You may make a new contact, you may not, but I know one thing. Even if you don't really talk, that person will remember you next time you're in the gym.
- **Cardio** – This can be hit or miss. If you come with someone, then this is easy, if not, I find most people zone out with headphones.
- **Entering and leaving** – I always seem to be holding the door for someone on the way in and out. Be cheerful and kind. Connection is not always words.

At the store (grocery, department, etc.)

- **Compliment someone** – You may notice someone has a great pair of shoes, a nice outfit, a cool T-shirt. When you're out and about, there are lots of opportunities for you to reach out to someone and make them feel good. You'll love how you feel afterwards too! (This is one of my go-to's. I love finding something that makes people smile.)
- **In line at the grocery store** – This is a great spot for compliments and general conversation. (Yes, the "How about this weather" still works!). I compliment people on well behaved children, or sometimes make comments about the food going on the conveyor belt after mine. That's the "Hmmm, can I come over to your house?" type of moment. Sometimes it is just saying "You doing alright today?" to the cashier.
- **At the store** – Whether you're just browsing or waiting to check out, you can compliment someone's purchase, talk about the weather, or simply smile and say hello.

Quick Responses That Still Show You Care

We've talked about how to send non-pushy texts, but responding matters just as much — sometimes even more. A short, respectful reply shows you value the person and sets the tone for the relationship.

Here are a few quick, no-pressure responses that communicate care without overcommitting:

- **"Sorry, I can't talk right now. I'll catch up with you when I can."**
  Direct and respectful. There's no dial tone anymore to warn someone they're interrupting, so telling them goes a long way.
- **"I'm in the car and can't return your call or text right now."**
  Most phones have an auto-reply for driving. Use it — it shows courtesy and keeps you safe.
- **"Let me get back to you in [timeframe]."**
  If you know when you'll be free, say so. If not, keep it general: *"I'll get back to you when I can."* Either way, you save them from wondering or chasing.
- **"Thank you" or "Appreciate you"**
  These are short, but long in feeling. They go a long way to show caring.
- **"Got your message, thanks! Will talk soon"**
  Something along those lines show that your communication wasn't forgotten, or worse – ignored.

The point isn't to give a full explanation — it's simply to acknowledge them. A short, clear response is one of the simplest ways to show someone they matter.

At Work

Work can feel even more intimidating than the outside world, but connection doesn't stop when you walk into the office. Since most of us spend the majority of our time here, it's also one of the best places to build strong rapport — making your work life both more productive and more enjoyable. The tools don't change, but the context does. At work, connection often carries higher stakes and bigger rewards, so it helps to use your skills in ways that are both positive and professional.

Keys to Working With Your Boss

Your boss is one of the most important people to build a strong connection with. It's not about sucking up, it's about understanding how they work, anticipating needs, and helping them succeed. When your boss wins, you usually win too.

Start here to begin building a productive relationship:

- **Be patient** – Build trust over time. Don't rush it.
- **Start with work** – Your easiest entry point is the work itself. That's your shared context.
- **Ask questions** – The more you clarify up front, the easier your job becomes. Make it a habit to confirm what success looks like.
- **Accept criticism** – This one's tough. But your boss's role includes giving feedback—and not all of it will feel warm and fuzzy.
- **Remember it's work** – Don't take everything personally. (This was a hard one for me).

Keys to Working With Admins

Admins often hold the keys to schedules, access, and organizational flow. Treat them with the respect they deserve—and more. Strong connections here can smooth your path and open doors in surprising ways.

Here are a few ways to get to know these important players:

- **Create opportunities** – If your boss needs something sent to an executive, offer to hand-deliver it. Make an effort to say hello and learn their names.
- **Stay curious** – Ask how long they've worked with their exec. What do they enjoy about it? What's one of the most interesting parts of the job?
- **Show kindness** – If you see them buried in work, offer a coffee run. Even the smallest gesture can leave a lasting impression.
- **Practice patience** – Exec calendars change on a dime. That open slot you were promised? It might disappear without warning. Don't take it personally—it's not about you.

Another key to thriving at work is adjusting to the culture around you. Every company — and every team — has its own rhythm and tone. The better you understand it, the easier it is to connect in ways that actually land.

Leadership Culture Check

Leaders set the tone for culture. Ask yourself: what cues are you giving your team? Respect, curiosity, and kindness spread quickly. So do negativity and indifference. Take stock of your impact, because people are taking theirs from you.

You can't really go anywhere until you have a firm idea of where you are, or where you've been. The same thing goes with culture. Here are a few questions to help you take stock:

- **Examine culture** – Do I know what kind of culture my team would say we have?
- **Establish ownership** – Is this culture mine—or did I inherit it?
- **Determine influencers** – Who are my cultural carriers? Are they aligned with the tone I want to set?
- **Evaluate impact** – What kind of ripple effect do my comments or requests typically have?
- **Get perspective** – When was the last time I actively sought feedback from someone far removed from me on the org chart?
- **Identify go-getters** – Do I have at least one "Bill" on my team? Or better yet—am I that Bill?

Respectful Responding

Responding is one of the simplest ways to show respect. Even a short reply goes a long way in building trust and showing people that they matter.

A quick text or short reply is often all it takes to stay accountable. Think of these as the work versions of *Quick Responses*. It lets people know you care enough to keep the connection alive. Here are some ready-to-use lines:

- "In a meeting — I'll call you back."
- "Can't talk now, but I'll check in later this week."
- "Saw this. Thanks. More soon."

If you have an instant communicator program at your company, you know that you get messages during meetings and other inconvenient times. Being able to be clear and respond will save you time and hassle down the road.

Of course, connection isn't just about responding — it's also about starting conversations that matter.

Let them Save Face

As I mentioned in the book, it's hard not to focus on the goal of being right. The problem is, that "win" can last far longer in memory if the other person ends up feeling embarrassed. The argument itself might be forgotten, but the way you made them feel can carry forward for years..

Being able to show **grace** isn't a skill you hear discussed much—if at all—in business. But if you want to keep a relationship, it's often the only way to do it. Grace means helping someone find a way to keep their dignity, even in defeat. This isn't about letting anyone win; it's about showing that the situation truly isn't more important than the person.

Try to utilize one of these methods in your next tense discussion:

- **Give them credit** - "You've brought up some good points that have given me things to consider."
- **Acknowledge the tension** - "I know this has been a tense discussion. I appreciate your partnership and willingness to bring up alternate options."
- **Bury the hatchet** - Once things cool, make a point to reconnect and clear the air—especially if you'll be working together often.
- **Apologize** – You may have inadvertently offended the person you're arguing with. If you even feel the slightest question of that, it's important to apologize for your part—even if you think it's only one percent your fault. *(This also works well with spouses, significant others, etc.)*
- **Include them** – Even if your idea is the one that prevailed, include your opposition to help it succeed. Just make sure the offer is genuine; if it feels like charity, it will backfire.

And one last thing—try to have the same grace when *you're* on the losing side of an argument.

Questions to Find Common Ground

A little small talk can go a long way when it's grounded in genuine curiosity. If you're not sure how to start, here are a few simple jumping-off points to find some common ground:

- Work experience – Where did they come from? What roles have they had? What did they study?
- Geography – Are they from here? Did they move for the job?
- Entertainment – What kind of music do they like? Do they read? Binge-watch anything? (I can't help but fire off 80's movie and music quotes myself)
- Sports – Do they follow any teams? Play anything themselves?
- Travel – Been anywhere interesting lately?

Sure, they may seem obvious, but sometimes those are the hardest to remember. And remember—the goal isn't to check boxes. This isn't a quiz. You're just opening doors to real conversation.

Translation/Jargon Check

When you're working across teams, it's easy to fall into the trap of only speaking your language. Here are a few quick ways to know if you're connecting—or just confusing:

- **Watch their faces and body language** – Are you getting nods or blank stares? Blank stares = time to translate (I've never had that happen.... Not).
- **Check the questions** – If all they ask is "What does that mean?" you might be in jargon mode. Worse still is no questions at all. Many people if they don't understand won't ask questions as they don't want to look dumb.
- **Flip the test** – Can they explain back your point in their words? If yes, you've landed it. Paraphrasing is not only useful, but polite and courteous.

- **Balance the airtime** – If you're talking 90% of the time, you're probably not learning their language. By the way, this is hard for me... I like to talk.

The sooner you understand each other, the faster and more efficiently you'll work together—not just on this project, but the next ones too.

And when you really want ideas to stick, nothing works better than a good story.

Storytelling 101

Stories build trust and make ideas stick. Don't overthink it—just be real. Even awkward or embarrassing stories can create connection faster than a polished pitch.

Stick to what you know. You speak most naturally and confidently when you're sharing your own experience. Don't try to impress, just be real. Keep these in mind:

- **Be relevant** – The right story at the wrong time is still the wrong story. At work, a short anecdote that ties to the task or goal is perfect. In social settings, read the room. Not every story fits every moment.
- **Be true** – The best stories are the ones that really happened. Whether they ended in triumph or disaster, honesty makes them relatable.
- **Circle back to a point or question** – A good story can make a point, ask a question, or invite someone else to share. Try closing with something like, "Has that ever happened to you?".
- **Use humor** – Embarrassing moments, small failures, or human quirks make great stories, especially when you can laugh at yourself. Humor builds trust and makes your story more memorable.

So, now if you're thinking, "I've got stories, but they're mostly awkward or embarrassing", don't worry. That might be your *best* advantage.

The Secret Door Isn't Just for Starters

We often think of sideways or support-staff relationships as early-career hacks — ways to get access when you're not yet senior. But the truth is, those "secret doors" never stop being useful. Even at the executive level, trust with assistants, coordinators, and peers can open doors you didn't even know existed.

The funny thing about these secret doors is that you build them yourself. Your relationships and actions forge shortcuts later in your career that you never could have planned for. How? Here are a few ways:

- **Help people** – If a colleague needs something that will only take you a few minutes, try to help right then — even if you're in the middle of something. Five minutes may not dent your work, but it could be crucial to theirs. People remember who helped them in a pinch, and when you're the one in need, those markers come back your way.
- **Share your knowledge** – Old-school thinking said to hoard expertise for job security. I subscribe to the opposite. Give your knowledge away, teach shortcuts, and help mold the next generation to be better, faster. You never know when someone you helped early on will be the person you're working with — or even working for — down the road.
- **Build relationships with powerful people** – Not many people stay in the same job forever. When you build strong ties with high-performing, respected people, they become advocates for you and your work — often far better than any résumé could.

- **Look sideways, not just up** – Some of the most valuable secret doors aren't executives — they're peers in other departments, colleagues you've collaborated with, or even people you've simply treated well along the way. Careers shift. Companies change. The teammate or colleague you helped today could be leading tomorrow.

Legacy

Thinking Long Term

Trust me, small connections aren't small—because with long-term relationships, each one is like a brick. On its own it doesn't look like much, but brick by brick, you're building something that can last a lifetime.

Here are a few practical ways to stay connected:

- **Start small** – Check in on people. Text them. Message them on social media. Email. Make a quick phone call. None of these are wrong.
- **Be patient** – Don't expect replies. People are busy, just like you. You may not hear back quickly. This isn't about parity; it's about caring.
- **Mark big moments** – Pay attention to birthdays, kids' birthdays, anniversaries, and even losses and struggles. Major life events matter deeply to people.
- **Be genuine** – Reach out because you care and you're interested, not just to check a box.

Water Your Network, Even When Nothing's Growing

Connections aren't just about quick wins — they're about planting seeds you may not see sprout for years — sometimes even a decade.

Types of connections worth making:

- **Career-experienced** – They've hit the potholes and can help you avoid them.
- **Well-connected** – They seem to know everyone, and over time, those introductions matter.

- **The bosses** – Senior leaders often appreciate curiosity and initiative when approached respectfully.
- **Everyone** – You never know where people will go or what they'll do. The more people you know, the more opportunities you'll have down the line.

And remember, not every connection pays off right away. That's okay. Stay in light touch. Send a note now and then, even when you don't 'need' anything. Because the opportunity that changes your life might be ten years down the line.

Keeping Your Network Flourishing

- **Play the long game** – A quick check-in once or twice a year is enough to keep many connections alive. Consistency matters more than frequency. People move in and out of our lives constantly—your check-in might reignite a connection at just the right time.
- **Mark it down** – Use birthdays, work anniversaries, or calendar reminders to prompt a simple message. LinkedIn is a great resource here since those notifications pop up automatically.
- **Keep it light** – You don't need deep conversations every time. A "thinking of you," "saw this and thought of you," or "congratulations on your work anniversary" shows you're paying attention. (Pro tip: skip LinkedIn's canned auto-replies—people notice the difference when you take five seconds to make it real.)
- **Trust the compound effect** – Over time, small touchpoints add up to real relationships. Not every connection will stick, but over years you'll build a circle of people you actually like reaching out to—and who like reaching out to you.

Reconnecting Years Later

Keeping your network not only growing but thriving is incredibly important. You never know how your connections may end up helping you down the line. Here's an example of how one of my connections paid off—ten years later.

Rod and I worked together over a decade ago. We were friendly—shared a few laughs, worked on a couple projects—but we didn't hang out outside of work after I left that company. What we did do was keep in touch now and then: an occasional call, a LinkedIn message, sometimes a text.

Fast-forward ten years.

Rod reached out. He was at a new company, they had an open role, and he thought I'd be a great fit. Because we'd stayed lightly connected, I wasn't just a name on a résumé—he remembered how I worked, and he trusted me enough to put my name forward.

I got the job.

Here's the kicker: that opportunity completely changed the direction of my career. And it all came from a connection I'd kept alive with small, simple touches over the years.

This wasn't the result of a brilliant networking campaign or a perfect follow-up cadence. I hadn't kept up very actively with Rod, and I wasn't expecting anything. But during the time we worked together, I built a friendly rapport with him. We had fun communicating, and I helped him develop a better understanding of technology. Rod remembered that.

We tend to think that only our close relationships matter—that unless we're actively nurturing a connection, it's lost. But this story reminds me that even loose ties, even casual connections, can come back around in powerful ways.

Never underestimate the impression you leave. And never underestimate the quiet value of being someone people want to reconnect with—even years down the road.

Keeping up with connections you've made at work is almost always a good idea. Like with Rod, you never know if you'll be working with, for, or introduced by someone who remembers you as a person—not just a résumé. That's the real power of the network people talk about so much.

The Legacy You Don't Intend to Leave

Legacy doesn't only come from your best moments. It also shows up in the ones where you're tired, stressed, or just done. Snapping at someone may feel small to you, but it might be the thing they remember all day—or longer.

You don't have to be perfect, but being aware that you leave a legacy even when frustrated gives you power. Sometimes your worst moment can become someone else's lasting impression of you. That, too, is legacy.

Ask yourself: what impression am I leaving right now?

Paying It Forward

One of the most meaningful ways to leave a legacy is to pass on what you've learned. This doesn't need to be formal mentorship or a big program with a capital "M." Small actions add up.

In the Office

- **Encourage growth** – Support someone earlier in their career.
- **Share contacts** – Offer an introduction that helps them get a foot in the door.

- **Offer guidance** – Give the advice you wish someone had given you at that stage.
- **Provide opportunities** – Give someone the chance to present and get noticed.
- **Teach skills** – Share the tips and tricks you've found helpful.
- **Empower improvement** – Let people improve processes, even if it replaces something you built. It's about what works best, not who gets credit.

Out of the Office

- **Make their day** – Brighten a stranger's day with a smile.
- **Practice politeness** – Open doors, help carry something heavy, or lend a hand when you see the chance.
- **Get to know people** – Learn the names and stories of the people who serve you (wait staff, clerks, retail employees).
- **Introduce others** – Connect people you think might get along.
- **Be dependable** – Offer help with pickups, house-sitting, or other small but meaningful favors.

These small steps can make big impacts for people. What feels small to you can land much bigger for someone else. People remember the ones who lifted them up, who noticed them, who gave them a boost when it mattered.

Your legacy isn't only the relationships you build for yourself — it's also the ones you help others build. When you invest in someone else's success, you create ripples that go far beyond your own circle.

And so ends this Field Guide. Use it as it was intended — come back to it for ideas, try what works, and jot your own into the margins.

I don't have the license on connecting.

I just hope what's here helps you along the way. Wherever your field takes you and whoever you meet, I wish you the best in the journey.

About the Author

Marc Zawrotny has spent more than thirty years in finance and technology leadership, helping companies navigate change while keeping people at the center of the process.

After realizing that connection is his superpower, he decided to write about connection, leadership, and the ways we build trust — lessons drawn from office meetings, water coolers and coffee shops.

When he isn't consulting or writing, Marc enjoys making people laugh, lifting weights, gaming, playing guitar and spending time with his wife, Melissa, and their family in Texas.

Reach Out is his first book.

www.ingramcontent.com/pod-product-compliance
Lightning Source LLC
Chambersburg PA
CBHW020539030426
42337CB00013B/907